Aligning Unevenly:
India and the United States

About the East-West Center

The East-West Center promotes better relations and understanding among the people and nations of the United States, Asia, and the Pacific through cooperative study, research, and dialogue. Established by the US Congress in 1960, the Center serves as a resource for information and analysis on critical issues of common concern, bringing people together to exchange views, build expertise, and develop policy options.

The Center's 21-acre Honolulu campus, adjacent to the University of Hawai'i at Mānoa, is located midway between Asia and the US mainland and features research, residential, and international conference facilities. The Center's Washington, DC, office focuses on preparing the United States for an era of growing Asia Pacific prominence.

The Center is an independent, public, nonprofit organization with funding from the US government, and additional support provided by private agencies, individuals, foundations, corporations, and governments in the region.

Policy Studies
an East-West Center series

Series Editors
Dieter Ernst and Marcus Mietzner

Description
Policy Studies presents original research on pressing economic and
political policy challenges for governments and industry across Asia,
and for the region's relations with the United States. Written for the
policy and business communities, academics, journalists, and the informed public, the peer-reviewed publications in this series provide
new policy insights and perspectives based on extensive fieldwork and
rigorous scholarship.

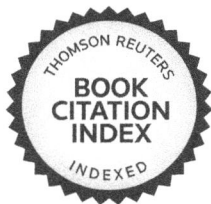

Policy Studies is indexed in the *Web of Science Book
Citation Index.* The *Web of Science* is the largest
and most comprehensive citation index available.

Notes to Contributors
Submissions may take the form of a proposal or complete manuscript.
For more information on the Policy Studies series, please contact the
Series Editors.

Editors, Policy Studies
East-West Center
1601 East-West Road
Honolulu, Hawai'i 96848-1601
Tel: 808.944.7197
Publications@EastWestCenter.org
EastWestCenter.org/PolicyStudies

Policy
Studies | 74

Aligning Unevenly:
India and the United States

Dinshaw Mistry

Aligning Unevenly: India and the United States
Dinshaw Mistry

ISSN 1547-1349 (print) and 1547-1330 (electronic)
ISBN 978-0-86638-272-4 (print) and 978-0-86638-273-1 (electronic)

The views expressed are those of the author(s) and not necessarily those of the East-West Center.

Print copies are available from Amazon.com. Free electronic copies of most titles are available on the East-West Center website, at EastWestCenter.org/PolicyStudies, where submission guidelines can also be found. Questions about the series should be directed to:

Publications Office
East-West Center
1601 East-West Road
Honolulu, Hawai'i 96848-1601
Tel: 808.944.7145
Fax: 808.944.7376
EWCBooks@EastWestCenter.org
EastWestCenter.org/PolicyStudies

In Asia, print copies of all titles, and electronic copies of select Southeast Asia titles, co-published in Singapore, are available from:

Institute of Southeast Asian Studies
30 Heng Mui Keng Terrace
Pasir Panjang Road, Singapore 119614
publish@iseas.edu.sg
bookshop.iseas.edu.sg

Cover: Official White House Photo by Pete Souza

Contents

List of Acronyms

ASEAN	Association of Southeast Asian Nations
BJP	Bharatiya Janata Party
BRICS	Brazil, Russia, India, China, and South Africa
CSC	Convention on Supplementary Compensation for Nuclear Damage
EU	European Union
FBI	Federal Bureau of Investigation (US)
GDP	gross domestic product
IAEA	International Atomic Energy Agency
km	kilometer
MTCR	Missile Technology Control Regime
MW	megawatt (of electricity)
NATO	North Atlantic Treaty Organization
NPT	(nuclear) Nonproliferation Treaty
NSG	Nuclear Suppliers Group
PPP	purchasing power parity

PSI	Proliferation Security Initiative
SUA	suppression of unlawful acts
UK	United Kingdom
UN	United Nations
US	United States
WMD	weapons of mass destruction

Executive Summary

During the early and mid-2000s, US policymakers anticipated that India could become one of America's closest global partners. A decade later, the question arises: Have New Delhi's policies on key strategic issues actually aligned strongly with US objectives, as would be typical of close partners? An analysis of twelve prominent issues in US-India relations offers answers to this question.

The analysis reaches five findings. First, New Delhi's policies on the issues converged, on the average, moderately with US objectives. On most of the issues, India's policies did not converge to the high extent typical of close allies, though they converged to a greater extent than skeptical perspectives would suggest.

Second, convergence was uneven across the issues: India's policies aligned with US objectives to a high or moderate-to-high extent on three issues—UN peacekeeping, nonproliferation export controls, and arms sales. They aligned to a moderate or low-to-moderate extent on six issues—China, Iran, Afghanistan, Indian Ocean security, Pakistan, and bilateral defense cooperation. And they aligned to a low or negligible extent on three issues—nuclear reactor contracts for US firms, nuclear arms control, and the war in Iraq. To be sure, on no issue—including the issues where convergence was negligible— did New Delhi take an anti-US position that would undermine US objectives.

Third, greater convergence between New Delhi's policies and US preferences often occurred slowly, over a period of years rather than months. Illustrating this, it took about five years for convergence to reach high levels on nonproliferation export controls, almost a decade for convergence to reach moderate-to-high levels on arms sales, and six years for convergence to move from negligible to low levels on nuclear deals for US firms.

Fourth, after the right-wing Bharatiya Janata Party came to power in 2014, New Delhi's policies on some issues did align better with US objectives—but the overall picture is still one of moderate, rather than high, alignment between New Delhi's policies and US strategic objectives.

Fifth, four factors explain the extent to which New Delhi's policies converged with and advanced US objectives: India's strategic interests, domestic political and economic factors, incentives and disincentives, and certain case-specific factors.

First, in several cases where the US objectives also furthered India's strategic interests—those of US arms sales to India, bilateral defense and security cooperation, Indian Ocean security, balancing China, stability in Afghanistan, and a peace process with Pakistan—India's policies did align with US objectives. However, they aligned mostly to a moderate or low-to-moderate rather than a high extent, because of domestic political and economic obstacles.

Second, domestic economic constraints and political impediments—both bureaucratic and legislative—reduced the extent to which New Delhi's policies aligned with US objectives. For instance, economic constraints prevented New Delhi from purchasing greater quantities of US arms, from more substantially modernizing its military forces to balance China, and from acquiring greater naval capabilities to play a larger role in Indian Ocean security. Political and bureaucratic factors also influenced these and additional cases. Thus, leftist opposition in the mid-2000s prevented India from increasing defense cooperation with the United States. Bureaucratic barriers in India's arms procurement process affected some US arms deals with India. Also, the Indian bureaucracy's preference for maintaining "strategic autonomy" hindered New Delhi from strongly aligning with Washington in balancing China and from deeper bilateral security cooperation. Moreover, domestic political obstacles were one factor holding back the India-Pakistan peace process in the early 2010s. And Indian legislative obstacles prevented US nuclear reactor sales to India.

Third, incentives and disincentives induced New Delhi to better align its policies with US interests. Thus, the disincentive of reduced US congressional support for the US-India civilian nuclear agreement influenced New Delhi to align with US preferences by strengthening export controls and by voting against Iran at the International Atomic Energy Agency.

Fourth, certain case-specific factors influenced New Delhi's policies. One such factor was the spoiler role played by Pakistan's security establishment and Pakistan-based militants, who reduced the extent to which India's policies aligned with and advanced US interests. Thus, Pakistan's support for the Afghan Taliban negated the potentially greater impact that Indian economic assistance could have had on state-building in Afghanistan. And militant groups significantly disrupted the India-Pakistan peace process in the late 2000s and early 2010s.

A second such factor relates to UN resolutions. In three cases—those of nonproliferation export controls, Iran, and UN peacekeeping—India better supported the preferred US policy when there was a UN resolution or UN backing on the issue. Further, in two instances—the war in Iraq and the Proliferation Security Initiative—the absence of a UN resolution undermined India's support for US preferences.

Looking ahead, and learning from the recent past, US policymakers could thus moderate their expectations about strategic relations with India. Rather than expecting New Delhi to become a military ally or a closely aligned partner, they should consider New Delhi to be a friendly strategic partner whose policies would align, on the average, moderately and partially with US strategic interests.

Aligning Unevenly:
India and the United States

Introduction

During the early and mid-2000s, US policymakers anticipated that India could become one of America's closest international partners and that this enhanced relationship with India was set to advance US interests. By the 2010s, however, while some analysts and policymakers remained optimistic about US-India relations, others questioned the initial enthusiasm about ties with India.[1] This contrast between optimists and skeptics gives rise to two important questions. First, have New Delhi's policies on key strategic issues actually aligned closely with US interests, as would be expected from close partners, or have India's policies not converged with US objectives, as skeptics of the US-India relationship suggest?[2] Second, what factors explain why New Delhi's policies converged with or diverged from US objectives? This study addresses these questions by examining New Delhi's policies on twelve issues in the US-India strategic dialogue.

The study finds that New Delhi's policies aligned, on the average, moderately and partially with US objectives. On most issues, they did not align with US objectives to the high extent typical of close partners, though they aligned better than the skeptical perspective would suggest. Relatedly, alignment was uneven across issue-areas: New Delhi's policies aligned with US objectives to a high or moderate-to-high extent on three issues—UN peacekeeping, nonproliferation export controls, and arms sales; to a moderate or low-to-moderate extent in six cases—China, Iran, Afghanistan, Indian Ocean security, Pakistan, and bilateral defense cooperation; and to a low or negligible extent in three areas—nuclear reactor contracts for US firms, nuclear arms control, and the 2003 war in Iraq. Just as significantly, even when New Delhi's policies aligned with US objectives, they took a long time—often several years—to do so.

Four main factors explain these outcomes, as noted in table 1 (and as illustrated in more detail in the rest of this study): New Delhi's strategic interests concerning the issue, domestic political and economic factors, incentives and disincentives, and certain case-specific factors (UN resolutions on some cases, and the spoiler role played by Pakistan-based militants and Pakistan's security establishment in two cases).

In general, and rather predictably, in many cases where the US objectives furthered India's strategic interests (such as by increasing its military and economic power versus its rivals), India's policies did converge with US objectives. However, even in such cases, they tended to converge only to a moderate rather than a high extent, largely because of domestic political and economic obstacles. Domestic economic constraints were especially relevant in the cases of China, arms sales, and Indian Ocean security, while domestic political obstacles were relevant in almost all the cases. Incentives and disincentives also influenced New Delhi to better align its policies with US objectives, especially in the cases of export controls and Iran. The following sections of this study elaborate upon these points. The study begins with a background on US-India relations, and then examines the case studies that illuminate the dynamics behind Indian policy alignment with US strategic interests.

US-India Relations: A Brief Overview

During the Cold War, Washington and New Delhi were often regarded as "estranged democracies." This was due to the fact that despite sharing some common interests, they had significant political differences over US support for Pakistan, India's tilt toward the Soviet Union, and India's remaining outside the nuclear Nonproliferation Treaty (NPT) (Gould and Ganguly 1992; Kux 1993; Limaye 1993; McMahon 1994; R. Chaudhuri 2014). In the post–Cold War era,

Table 1. Factors Causing Indian Policy Convergence (+) or Divergence (-) with US Objectives on Issues

Factors	India's Strategic Interests	Domestic Political Obstacles	Economic Constraints	Incentives or Disincentives	Other*	India's Policy Convergence with US Objectives
Issue						
Nonproliferation Export Controls		-		+	UNR (+)	Low (early 2000s) => High (2010s)
UN Peacekeeping				+	UNR (+)	High
Arms Sales	+	-	-			Low (early 2000s) => Moderate-to-High (2010s)
Balancing China	+	-	-			Low-to-Moderate / Moderate
Indian Ocean Security	+	-	-			Moderate
Iran	-	-		+		Moderate
Afghanistan	+	-			Pak (-)	Moderate
Pakistan	+	-			Pak (-)	Low (early 2000s) => Moderate (mid-2000s) => Low-to-Moderate (late 2000s & early 2010s)
Defense Cooperation	+	-				Low-to-Moderate
Nuclear Arms Control	-	-		+		Low
Nuclear Reactor Contracts	+	-				Negligible (early 2010s) => Low (in 2015)
War in Iraq		-			No UNR (-)	Negligible

*Other factors—UNR: UN Resolutions; Pak: Pakistan-based militants and Pakistan's security agencies

Washington and New Delhi sought to improve their relations. For instance, India's economic liberalization offered greater investment and export opportunities for US firms (Schaffer 2009; Vickery 2011). Further, the Clinton administration began a limited defense dialogue with India. However, this period of improved strategic ties was not without its problems, and it culminated in a major setback: India's 1998 nuclear tests resulted in US sanctions on India.

In the 2000s, the Bush administration sought stronger strategic relations with India to balance a rising China, and because it expected to work with India on broader regional and international security challenges. It sought to "intensify collaboration with India on the whole range of issues that currently confront the international community" (Blackwill 2005, 9). India's democratic credentials made a partnership with it especially appealing.[3] For its part, India's government—then led by the Bharatiya Janata Party (BJP)—emphasized that the "litmus test" for a strategic partnership with Washington was a settlement of their nuclear differences. In July 2005—the BJP government had then given way to one led by the centrist Congress Party—the Bush administration accommodated New Delhi's position. Washington agreed to recognize India's nuclear weapons status and to remove longstanding embargoes on civilian nuclear trade with India. The two sides also signed a ten-year defense cooperation agreement in June 2005. Three years later, after protracted talks between the US and Indian governments, and between each government and its respective legislature, Washington and New Delhi formally signed their nuclear agreement—an agreement that US policymakers hoped would "help transform the partnership between the world's oldest and the world's largest democracy" (Rice 2006).

The US-India civilian nuclear agreement aimed to 'transform the partnership between the world's oldest and the world's largest democracy'

Subsequently, under the Obama administration, the two sides held annual strategic dialogue meetings where they discussed bilateral relations at the highest political levels, and President Obama visited India in 2010. Still, during the early 2010s, the prior optimism about US-India relations was gradually replaced by skepticism, partly because New Delhi did not award lucrative combat aircraft and nuclear reactor contracts to US firms, and because of Indian misperceptions about the Obama administration's engagement of China and Pakistan.[4] This skepticism diminished after a new BJP-led government assumed office in 2014 and brought some improvements to the relationship. The personal chemistry between Prime Minister Modi and President Obama was strong; President Obama was the chief guest at India's January 2015 Republic Day celebrations, while Prime Minister Modi visited the United States in September 2014 and September 2015; and Washington and New Delhi upgraded their annual strategic dialogue to a strategic and commercial dialogue in 2015. Despite these developments, questions remain about the strength of the alignment between New Delhi's foreign policy and US strategic interests.

The Analytical Framework: Cases and Factors in US-India Relations

Contemporary writings on US-India ties provide much empirical information on the main issues in the bilateral relationship (Kronstadt and Pinto 2013; Brookings Institution 2015). However, they do not test the historical record against the main analytical questions raised in this study—the questions of how well New Delhi's policies on the issues aligned with US objectives, and why or why not. To be sure, there is nothing surprising about US and Indian policies not always aligning (the policies of America's other partners and allies often do not align with US preferences either). Also, the notion of the United States and India being close partners or natural allies could be considered as diplomatic rhetoric. Yet such rhetoric does influence policy making, and it is therefore important to test it against the empirical record.

This study undertakes such a test by examining twelve prominent cases in the US-India strategic dialogue. It examines six of these in some depth: the regional issue of China's rise; broader international security issues of nonproliferation export controls and Iran's nuclear program; and bilateral issues concerning arms sales, defense and security cooperation, and nuclear contracts for US firms. Thereafter, to probe whether the factors influencing these cases are more generalizable, it briefly examines six additional cases—the regional challenges of Afghanistan, Pakistan, and Indian Ocean security, and the international security issues of UN peacekeeping, nuclear arms control, and Iraq.

This selection of cases—covering the regional, international, and bilateral domains—ensures that the study is not narrowly limited to just one of these arenas. Also, the strategic issues selected were all formally or implicitly part of US-India dialogues, and Washington and New Delhi discussed most of the issues over prolonged periods of time; they were not short-term, one-time events, such as a single UN vote on a specific issue. Further, the study excludes strategic issues for which Washington did not request major actions from New Delhi or did not engage it in sustained discussions—issues such as the Russia-Ukraine conflict and the crisis in Syria in the 2010s. Furthermore, since the study focuses on strategic issues, it excludes economic issues (though it does examine arms deals that were both strategic and economic, and nuclear reactor contracts that followed from a strategic agreement—the US-India civilian nuclear agreement). The analysis examines the period from the early 2000s to the time of writing (2015), when Washington actively sought a partnership with India, and when many American decision makers and analysts anticipated that, as the US dialogue with India advanced, New Delhi's actions would better align with US objectives.

For each case, the study assesses whether New Delhi's policies converged with US objectives to a high, moderate, low, negligible, or negative extent. Negligible convergence includes no convergence or simply abstaining from the issue, but is distinct from negative convergence. Negative convergence is defined as active opposition toward US policy (France and Germany's active opposition to the 2003 Iraq war is an example of negative policy convergence with US preferences). Convergence is measured in two ways. One is in comparison to other countries. For example, if India's policies converged with US objectives to the same extent as those of the countries most strongly aligned with the United States on the issue, convergence would be classified as high. A second approach looks at all items in the discussed issue-area and assesses whether India's policies converged with US objectives on almost all the particular items in this arena (high convergence), about half the items (moderate convergence), just a few items (low convergence), or almost none or none of the items (negligible convergence).

Two analytical caveats should be noted. First, this study broadly interprets policy alignment to include instances where a deliberate effort is made to align policy as well as instances of overlap where shared interests bring about similar policies. Second, policy alignment is distinct from policy effectiveness—strictly speaking, the concept of whether India's policy is ultimately effective in advancing US interests is different from the concept of whether India's policy initially aligns with US preferences. However, these two concepts can sometimes coincide. This paper adopts a broad definition of alignment to include policy effectiveness in cases where the two concepts are closely related.

The study also analyzes the principal factors that influenced New Delhi's policies on the cases—strategic considerations, domestic factors, and incentives and disincentives. First, on strategic grounds, New Delhi's policies would be most likely to converge with US objectives when the US objectives advance India's strategic interests—defined narrowly as increasing India's military capabilities and political options versus its rivals China and Pakistan, reducing the security threat from these rivals, increasing India's capabilities to tackle other security challenges, and increasing its economic strength.

Second, domestic economic and political factors influence New Delhi's policies. Thus, its policies would be expected to better align with US objectives when there are a) few economic constraints and b) few domestic political obstacles (both bureaucratic and legislative) to pursuing such policies. Domestic political obstacles influenced the cases in this study in a number of ways. To begin with, leftist parties, upon whom India's government relied to remain in office in the mid-2000s, opposed pro-US policies on issues ranging from export controls to Iran to China. Correspondingly, right-wing parties opposed certain aspects of nuclear arms control and peace talks with Pakistan when they were in opposition. Moreover, particular bureaucratic factors influenced some cases—for example, arms procurement rules influenced India's arms imports from the United States. Finally, the Indian bureaucracy's position on maintaining "strategic autonomy"—a position stemming from India's legacy of nonalignment and aversion to Cold War alliance blocs—formed a broader obstacle.[5] As a result, the bureaucracy opposed tighter security coordination with the United States and instead preferred flexible interactions typical of a "strategic partnership." (This term has been defined by Indian officials as a bilateral relationship that promotes policy convergence in issues of mutual interest without stronger alliance-type commitments [Sibal 2012]).[6] In a similar vein, India's foreign policy community remained wary of unilateral US foreign policy initiatives, but was less opposed to US initiatives that were backed by UN resolutions.

> *The Indian bureaucracy sought to maintain 'strategic autonomy'; it opposed tighter security coordination with the United States and instead preferred flexible interactions typical of a 'strategic partnership'*

Third, incentives and disincentives influence New Delhi's policies—India's policies would be expected to align well with US objectives when there is an incentive to align, or there is a disincentive to not align, with the US objective. These incentives and disincentives—offered by the United States or other entities—could be formally included in a deal on an issue; could be informally linked to a deal; or could be ambiguous and implied rather than explicitly linked to an issue. In combination, the above factors influenced New Delhi's policies on important cases, as will be shown in detail below.

China

Balancing China was a major reason behind US efforts to engage India since the early 2000s. Reflecting this balancing impulse before the Bush administration was elected to office, Condoleezza Rice noted that the United States "should pay closer attention to India's role in the regional balance [in Asia]. . . . India is an element in China's calculation, and it should be in America's, too" (Rice 2000). Echoing similar views in the mid-2000s, Undersecretary of State Nicholas Burns noted that "there is a tremendous strategic upside to our growing engagement with India" because such engagement held "real promise for the global balance of power" (Burns 2007, 131). As it turned out, New Delhi did pursue policies to balance China, but to an extent between low-to-moderate and moderate rather than high.

Balancing has two components—internal, related to building up national military capabilities, and external, involving partnerships with other states (Paul, Wirtz, and Fortman 2014). India pursued both approaches to balancing China (Smith 2014; Montgomery 2013). New Delhi's internal balancing had three dimensions. First, India increased its military forces in its northeastern sector bordering China. Thus, in the mid-2000s, it authorized the acquisition of two mountain divisions, the construction of border roads, and the reactivation of seven advanced landing grounds in this area (however, few of these projects were complete by 2015; Sethi 2015). It also fielded Mi-17 attack helicopters, Su-30 combat aircraft, and Brahmos cruise missiles in the region. Further, in 2013, it authorized plans for expanding the above mountain divisions into a new mountain strike corps of ninety thousand soldiers by 2020, at a cost of US$10.6 billion (though this plan was subsequently downsized).

Second, India enlarged its naval fleet, which gave it better capabilities versus China. The Indian navy acquired 15 frigates and destroyers in the 2000s and early 2010s, and was building or planned to start building another 15 such vessels in the mid-2010s.[7] Further, in 2014, it acquired an aircraft carrier—a thirty-year-old refurbished Russian vessel—to replace its sixty-year-old carrier that was nearing retirement. It was also building a second carrier that would be commissioned around 2018–20. In addition, it acquired a division-sized amphibious force and related sealift capability by obtaining a US-supplied amphibious vessel that could carry 1,000 troops and six helicopters; three tank-landing ships that could carry 500 troops and 10 tanks; and two new fleet tankers to augment two existing tankers. To be sure, the Indian naval expansion was aimed not at China but at protecting Indian Ocean sea-lanes through which much of India's trade and oil transits. And it would likely not give India the capability to conduct major sustained operations in the East and South China Seas. Yet it would enable India to impose limited pressure on Chinese assets in, and trade transiting through, the Indian Ocean and the Malacca Straits; and to better protect Indian (as well as US and other) shipping against Chinese pressure in these regions (Scott 2013; Mohan 2012; Brewster 2012).

Third, India developed a better nuclear deterrent versus China. In the 2000s, it did not have missiles that could strike China's major cities from secure sites in eastern and central India. However, it developed such capabilities after it began testing the 3,000 kilometer (km) range Agni-3 (since 2006), the 4,000 km range Agni-4 (since 2010), and the 5,000 km range Agni-5 (since 2012).

In terms of external balancing, New Delhi increased its defense and security interactions with other Asia-Pacific states, as well as with the United States in Asia. These interactions were somewhat limited and could not, by themselves, facilitate large-scale military pressure against China. But they offered defensive capabilities against Chinese political and military pressure in regional crises, especially when deployed together with the military forces of other states. Concretely, India's external balancing of China took place in four main areas.

First, New Delhi undertook a number of military exercises with the United States in Asia. The annual US-India Malabar naval exercises, which involved just one or two warships from each country in the early 2000s, grew to involve three to five warships from each country by the mid-2000s, and included US and Indian aircraft carriers during some years. They also involved Japanese, Australian, and Singaporean naval vessels in 2007, and Japanese vessels in 2009, 2014, and 2015. In addition, Washington and New Delhi formally affirmed the synergies between their security strategies in the Asia-Pacific, noting that "India's 'Act East Policy' and the United States' rebalance to Asia provide opportunities for India, the United States, and other Asia-Pacific countries to work closely" toward stability in the Asia-Pacific (The White House 2015a). (New Delhi's "Act East" policy was a rhetorical extension of its "Look East" policy, pursued since the 1990s, whereby its foreign policy establishment gave greater attention to East Asia and Southeast Asia.)

Second, India advanced bilateral defense interactions with some countries in China's vicinity, especially Singapore and Vietnam. India and Singapore began an annual Defense Policy Dialogue in 2003; India provided Singapore's army and air force with training facilities on Indian territory; the two countries conducted joint army and air force exercises in India; and they conducted annual naval exercises (Suryanarayan 2013). India and Vietnam signed a defense cooperation agreement in 2000 under which India offered spare parts and servicing for Vietnam's Soviet-era aircraft and naval vessels (this helped Vietnam to maintain a viable navy). The Indian navy also increased its port calls in Vietnam, making 17 such visits from 2001 to 2013 (Collin 2013).

Third, India initiated bilateral defense and security interactions with US allies. Most significantly, it developed a strategic partnership with Japan that had a small defense component (which was formalized in a Joint Declaration on Security Cooperation in 2008). This involved defense and foreign ministers' meetings, as well as additional ministerial-level and military-to-military talks, where the two sides discussed cooperation in protecting the sea lanes, disaster relief, and peacekeeping. India and Japan also undertook a cybersecurity dialogue; held bilateral naval exercises in 2012 and 2013 (these augmented their abovementioned multilateral exercises with the United States); conducted coast guard exercises

> *India initiated bilateral defense and security interactions with US allies; most significantly, it developed a strategic partnership with Japan that had a small defense component*

involving one to two vessels from each country since 2000; and discussed a US$1.6 billion sale of 12–15 Japanese amphibious patrol aircraft to India. In 2014, they began a dialogue of their national security advisors, and, during Prime Minister Modi's September 2014 visit to Japan, they pledged to advance their security dialogue. The following year, during Prime Minister Abe's visit to India, the two sides announced that Japan would participate regularly in the Malabar naval exercises and also reaffirmed their positions on the freedom of navigation in the oceans.[8] In addition, Japan agreed, after years of tough negotiations, to a civilian nuclear deal with India. Further, New Delhi participated in annual trilateral security discussions with Tokyo and Washington—the seventh trilateral in 2015 was upgraded to involve their foreign ministers.

New Delhi also undertook limited security interactions with America's other Asian allies, South Korea and Australia. India and South Korea signed a five-year defense cooperation agreement in 2010, and, in 2013, India planned to purchase eight Korean minesweepers for US$1 billion, but later cancelled this contract after corruption allegations. India and Australia held their first joint naval exercise, involving three ships from each country, in 2015. That year, India, Japan, and Australia also held their first trilateral meeting.

Fourth, India increased its participation in multilateral Asian regional security institutions such as the Association of Southeast Asian Nations (ASEAN) Regional Forum, which India joined in 1996, and the East Asia Summit, established in 2005. These ASEAN-led initiatives built solidarity between New Delhi and East and Southeast Asian states; provided them with mutually supportive diplomatic options in any crisis with China; and enabled them to reiterate their positions on regional security issues such as the peaceful resolution of disputes and the freedom of navigation in the seas.[9]

In sum, India's internal and external balancing initiatives dovetailed with the US interest of balancing China, but to an extent between low-to-moderate and moderate rather than high, for three principal reasons. The first relates to economic constraints. China's economy was considerably larger than India's and also grew faster than India's. Illustrating this, the ratio of Chinese to Indian gross domestic product (GDP, measured by purchasing power parity [PPP]) increased from 1.68 in 2000 to 2.3 in 2012 and 2.4 in 2014 (when China's GDP was US$18.03 trillion compared to India's US$7.4 trillion). Consequently, China could afford military forces and a military budget that remained substantially larger than India's, as shown in tables 2 and 3. This does not mean that China has a military advantage versus

Table 2. Military Expenditures for China and India (US$, billion)

	2005		2010		2014	
	India	China	India	China	India	China
Official defense budget	18	30	31	78	38	136
Baseline defense spending including off-budget items	24	45	43	113	-	-
PPP-adjusted baseline defense spending	45	69	88	138	-	-

Source: 2005 and 2010 figures are from Heginbotham and Gilroy (2012), who also computed the baseline defense spending value including paramilitary forces, arms imports, defense research and development, and subsidies to defense industries. Such spending as a percent of GDP was 2.96–3.02 percent for India and 1.97–1.98 percent for China. Figures from 2014 are the official national defense budgets which do not report baseline defense spending.

India along their border, however. In the eastern sector of the India-China border, India's air force can likely attain air superiority and Indian army units are quantitatively and qualitatively superior to Chinese forces (the bulk of Indian army and air force assets are still focused on Pakistan). In terms of naval forces, China focuses on the East and South China Seas and the Western Pacific and thus cannot simultaneously project a large naval force in the Indian Ocean region. Still, China's larger overall economy and larger military forces give it advantages in any war of attrition versus India.

The second factor that led to moderate, rather than high, levels of convergence was related to India's bureaucracy restricting the scope

Table 3. Military Forces in China and India, 2013–14

	China	India
Active military forces	2.28 million	1.32 million
Tanks	6,840	2,870
Artillery pieces	13,000	9,700
Submarines	65: 61 tactical and 4 carrying nuclear missiles	12, all tactical (plus 1 intended to carry nuclear missiles undergoing trials)
Principal naval vessels	70: 15 destroyers, 54 frigates, and 1 twenty-five-year-old ex-Soviet aircraft carrier used as a training vessel	24: 11 destroyers, 12 frigates, and 1 thirty-year-old ex-Soviet aircraft carrier (with a second sixty-year-old carrier near retirement)
Smaller naval patrol and coastal vessels	210	84
Aircraft	2,100 combat capable:* including 840 fighters, 540 fighter-ground attack, 320 transport planes, and 90 bombers	870 combat capable:* including 63 fighters, 730 fighter-ground attack, and 230 transport planes

Source: IISS (2014)
*Some 600 of the 840 Chinese fighters are obsolete Chinese-built versions of the Soviet Mig-19 and Mig-21; China's 200 other fighters, and most of its 540 fighter-ground attack planes, are more modern systems acquired in the first decade of the 2000s. India's 63 Mig-29 fighters and 200 Su-30 fighter-ground attack planes are relatively modern systems; its other fighter-ground attack aircraft include 50 Mirage-2000s, 100 Jaguars, 200 aging Mig-21s, and 100 aging Mig-27s.

of security interaction with the United States and with Asia-Pacific states. Analysts observed that, in the early 2010s, New Delhi "double downed on its autonomist leanings" because it "resisted participating in major multi-service combined exercises [with the United States] that prepare for high-end operational missions," "turned down a series of foundational pacts that would have enhanced logistics and battle-group networking," and "opted to strip out tactical interoperability aids (high-end electronics and avionics suites) while purchasing US-origin platforms (P-8I and C-130J aircraft)" (Gupta 2014). Simply put, India's foreign policy bureaucracy remained inclined toward a "nonalignment 2.0" approach of eschewing alliance-type initiatives directed at other countries; as a result, it limited India's external balancing initiatives versus China.

The third constraint has been strategic. While New Delhi pursued external and internal balancing to hedge against any deterioration in relations with China, it also sought to avert such deterioration by advancing political and economic ties with China. (Thus, it did not pursue "hard balancing" against China.) In the economic realm, China became one of India's four largest trading partners.[10] Politically, despite a downturn in Sino-Indian relations from 2005 to the early 2010s (coinciding with US engagement of India through a civilian nuclear agreement), New Delhi and Beijing sought to normalize ties through several heads-of-government visits and six strategic dialogue meetings involving their senior ministers.[11] Further, while India confronted China on troop incursions—between 2010 and August 2014, it counted 1,612 Chinese troop incursions into Indian territory according to a Ministry of Home Affairs report to the Indian Parliament—it also accommodated Chinese concerns that India not join multilateral military initiatives directed against China. Illustrating this, China reacted strongly to the 2007 Quadrilateral Initiative, in which the United States, India, Australia, and Japan held ad hoc discussions on Asian security and conducted a joint naval exercise; hence, New Delhi refrained from further multilateral naval exercises in Indian waters for the next several years, though Indian naval vessels continued participating in these exercises outside Indian waters. Finally, Prime Minister Modi's May 2015 visit to China largely confirmed both sides' preferences to normalize their bilateral relations. During this visit, the two sides found no solutions to their longstanding boundary dispute; however, they signed economic investment agreements worth US$20 billion and established a military hotline to prevent border skirmishes from escalating.

Overall, then, while New Delhi balanced China's rise in several strategic and political arenas, it did so to a low-to-moderate or moderate extent rather than to the high extent that some US policymakers and analysts had assumed it would.

> *While New Delhi balanced China's rise in several strategic and political arenas, it did so to a moderate extent*

Nonproliferation Export Controls

In the early 2000s, the Bush administration formally asked India to tighten its nonproliferation export controls as a prerequisite for technology transfers and civilian nuclear cooperation. In particular, it wanted New Delhi to strengthen its domestic laws on export controls and act on five related international initiatives: four multilateral regimes—the Nuclear Suppliers Group (NSG), the Missile Technology Control Regime (MTCR), the Australia Group restricting chemical transfers, and the Wassenaar Arrangement on transfers of conventional arms and related technologies—as well as the Proliferation Security Initiative (PSI). New Delhi's policies aligned with these US objectives to a low extent in the early 2000s, when it had less stringent national export controls; moderately in the mid-2000s, when it strengthened its national controls and gradually adhered to the NSG and the MTCR; and to a high extent by the early 2010s, when it also supported the Wassenaar Arrangement and Australia Group.

In terms of national export controls, New Delhi adopted formal legislation (the Weapons of Mass Destruction Prohibition Act, also called the WMD Act) in 2005 and took steps to enforce export controls. For example, India's Directorate General for Foreign Trade, which issues licenses for items on its export control list, held outreach meetings with Indian industry exporters. In the late 2000s, India's government further tightened its national export controls, and placed a renewed focus on enforcement and on outreach to industry, through its Export Controls and Border Security program. And, in 2010, it amended its Foreign Trade Act to tighten controls on the transfer and transit of dual-use technologies and services.

As far as the MTCR and NSG were concerned, New Delhi harmonized its control lists with, and announced its intention to adhere to, these regimes in July 2005. Yet it did not formally adhere to them for another three years, in part because it wanted the regimes to consider India as a partner and not a target. It ultimately adhered to the regimes in September 2008, just ahead of a US legislative vote on the civilian nuclear agreement.

New Delhi did not take substantial action on the Wassenaar Arrangement and the Australia Group until the 2010s. While it had national legislation to control the exports of dual-use chemicals, it still stated, in late 2005, that it was not prepared to harmonize its control lists with those of the Australia Group and the Wassenaar Arrangement (US Embassy 2005). It only changed its stance in the early 2010s when it sought membership in the four multilateral regimes (Nayan 2011). Thus, ahead of President Obama's November 2010 visit to India, Washington removed nine Indian defense and space-related organizations from its Entity List, and agreed to support India's membership in the four multilateral export control regimes.[12] In subsequent years, New Delhi actively engaged with the four regimes and sought to join them.[13]

New Delhi's position toward the PSI (an initiative launched by the United States in 2003 to interdict ships and aircraft suspected of carrying nuclear, chemical, or missile technology) was even more complex. Washington had urged New Delhi to support the initiative since early 2004, but New Delhi stalled on the US request. In 2005, New Delhi suggested that it would only join PSI if it became a member of the PSI core group that formulates PSI policies. It then opposed NPT-related language in the 2005 Protocols to the Convention for the Suppression of Unlawful Acts (SUA) against the Safety of Maritime Navigation. In the mid and late 2000s, New Delhi remained outside PSI despite US efforts to address the above objections.[14] Nevertheless, it still acted in accordance with PSI: it participated in PSI events as an observer, denied overflight permission to a North Korean plane en route to Iran in August 2008, and boarded a North Korean vessel headed to the Middle East in August 2009. Yet Indian officials continued to have concerns about how PSI fitted with the legal framework of the United Nations and about operational issues such as whether India could interdict Chinese ships suspected of carrying contraband (Schaffer and Rohlfing 2011).

A combination of domestic political factors and international incentives account for India's above approach to export controls. First, leftist parties, whose support India's government required to remain in office in the mid-2000s, strongly opposed Indian endorsement of PSI on the grounds that it represented excessive alignment with the United States. (The left did not oppose India's position on the four multilateral export control regimes because India's government framed these as part of India's obligations under UN Security Council Resolution 1540 rather than as part of a deal with the United States.) Indeed, this leftist opposition was so strong that it caused New Delhi to formally remain outside PSI at the time.

Second, India's bureaucracy raised several technical objections to PSI that were noted above; this caused New Delhi to not formally join PSI in the 2010s (by this time, the leftist opposition factor had become irrelevant since India's government did not then depend on the left to remain in office). Bureaucratic factors also influenced India's decisions on the Australia Group and Wassenaar Arrangement. In the mid and late 2000s, India's bureaucracy did not support joining these regimes, in part because India would not gain significant benefits from doing so and because Indian defense and space entities were still subject to US technology transfer restrictions. However, in 2010, after US-India track-II dialogues on the topic, Washington better addressed New Delhi's concerns and India's bureaucracy then looked favorably at the Australia Group and the Wassenaar Agreement (Schaffer and Rohlfing 2011). Even then, in the early 2010s, India's bureaucracy still created obstacles by seeking to join all four regimes simultaneously, while each regime had separate technical criteria for membership. This Indian position hindered its admission into each regime.

Third, incentives repeatedly influenced India's position on the multilateral export control regimes. In 2005, the major US incentive of civilian nuclear cooperation influenced India's government to expeditiously adopt its WMD Act and agree to adhere to the MTCR and NSG. Conversely, the disincentives were also high, because if New Delhi did not take these steps, Washington would not have agreed to civilian nuclear cooperation with India. In 2008, the follow-on incentive of US congressional authorization of civilian nuclear cooperation influenced India's government to finally adhere to the MTCR and NSG. And in the 2010s, two sets of incentives influenced New Delhi to actively engage the four multilateral regimes—a) the easing of US restrictions on Indian defense and space entities and b) the prospect of increased international prestige and status through membership in the regimes. In substantive policy terms, however, the incentives were highly disproportional, especially in the mid-2000s—Washington was then offering New Delhi a huge incentive, in the form of reversing major US nonproliferation policies and giving India a civilian nuclear deal, in return for relatively easier Indian action on export controls.

> *In 2005, the major US incentive of civilian nuclear cooperation influenced India's government to expeditiously adopt some nonproliferation export control measures*

To summarize, export controls should have been an easy case of converging US and Indian interests—India's government should have been able to quickly strengthen its national export controls and adhere to the four multilateral export control regimes in 2005. Yet, while New Delhi then acted on national export controls and on two of the multilateral regimes, it only sought full engagement with all four regimes in the early 2010s. Domestic political factors and incentives and disincentives explain New Delhi's slow but gradually increasing policy alignment with US preferences on these export control regimes.

Iran

In the 2000s and 2010s, as part of its effort to contain and impose nuclear-related sanctions on Iran, Washington urged New Delhi to act on several issues concerning Iran. It desired that New Delhi curb defense and political ties with Iran, vote against Iran at the International Atomic Energy Agency (IAEA), end participation in the Iran-Pakistan-India gas pipeline project, and reduce oil purchases from Tehran. Eventually, New Delhi's policies converged with these US preferences to a moderate extent overall, but the pattern was not consistent across the various issues: policies converged to a high extent on defense and specific nuclear issues, initially to a low extent and then to a moderate-to-high extent on energy issues, and did not converge on political issues.

On specific nuclear issues, New Delhi's actions aligned to a high extent with US preferences. Most importantly, New Delhi voted against Tehran at the IAEA meetings in November 2005, February 2006, November 2009, and November 2011.

On defense issues, New Delhi's policies initially deviated from, but then aligned to a high extent with, US preferences. In the early 2000s, New Delhi was considering small-scale defense interaction with Tehran, such as training Iranian officers and supplying spare parts and servicing for Iran's Russian-origin T-72 tanks, Kilo submarines, and Mig-29 fighters; it also conducted a small joint naval maneuver with Iran in 2003 (Kumaraswamy 2008; Pant 2007; Fair 2007). New Delhi ended these activities by the mid-2000s with only insignificant exceptions. Indian foreign policy officials then accepted the US position that even limited Indian technical assistance to Iran, such as servicing its Kilo submarines, could threaten US military forces in the Persian Gulf.

On energy issues, New Delhi's policies initially did not converge with US preferences but, after a few years, they aligned to a high extent on gas and moderately on oil. On the gas pipeline, despite objections from the Bush administration and the US Congress, New Delhi participated in several rounds of pipeline talks with Iran and Pakistan in the mid-2000s. Eventually, however, while Pakistan and Iran signed a pipeline contract in 2009, New Delhi did not sign that contract. This was not specifically in response to US requests, but because Iran, Pakistan, and India still had differences over the price, tariff, and location of the gas pipeline; because of instability in Baluchistan through which the pipeline would pass; and due to the setback in Pakistan-India relations after the November 2008 terrorist attacks in Mumbai. Later, New Delhi also held back on another gas investment in Iran, in the Farzad-B oil and gas field.

Concerning oil imports, New Delhi moderately aligned with US oil sanctions against Iran that had tightened in 2010–11. It cut its Iranian oil imports by half (from 21.8 million tons in 2009–10 to 11 million tons in 2013–14), but it did so gradually, by about 16 percent between 2009 and 2011, 25 percent the following year, and 16 percent the next year. (Such cuts by India, that accounted for 10-15 percent of Iran's oil exports, and by all other major purchasers of Iranian oil, helped put pressure on Iran to reach the Vienna nuclear agreement in July 2015.)

In the political arena, however, New Delhi did not align with US preferences and instead maintained high-level diplomatic exchanges with Tehran. India-Iran relations were advancing in 2003, when the two sides announced a "strategic partnership" and President Khatami visited India, but were set back by India's November 2005 and February 2006 votes against Iran at the IAEA. Subsequently, demonstrating New Delhi's strong efforts toward normalization with Tehran, India's cabinet ministers for external affairs, petroleum, and water resources, its minister of state for external affairs, and its foreign secretary all visited Iran in 2007. Moreover, President Ahmadinejad visited India in April 2008. (These diplomatic visits enabled India's government to demonstrate to domestic critics that it was standing up to Washington in maintaining an independent foreign policy on Iran.) In addition, Indian delegations, often led by the external affairs minister, visited Iran every other year since the late 2000s for meetings of the India-Iran Joint Commission (addressing economic, technological, and cultural cooperation). High-level India-Iran interactions continued in the 2010s, with Iran's foreign minister visiting New Delhi in February 2014 to "open a new chapter" in relations with India.[15]

A combination of strategic reasons, domestic political considerations, and incentives and disincentives explain why some of New Delhi's policies on Iran diverged from Washington's preferences. In terms of strategic regional security considerations, strong ties with Iran gave India a) the ability to geopolitically encircle Pakistan and b) a vital route for transporting heavy supplies into Afghanistan through the Iranian port of Chabahar (Aspen Institute India 2012). Further, Iran provided a significant 16 percent of India's oil imports in the mid-2000s, and New Delhi was reluctant to shift entirely to Sunni Arab suppliers (who provided over two-thirds of India's oil imports) because of their ties with Pakistan. These Indian strategic interests in maintaining relations with Tehran diverged from the US strategic objective of containing Iran.

In the domestic political arena, two factors affected India's Iran policy in the 2000s. First, India's Congress Party was concerned about losing the support of Muslim—and particularly Shiite—voters if it were seen as pursuing a pro-US and anti-Iran foreign policy. Its concerns were heightened because some Muslim organizations had mobilized, along with leftist parties and a regional party, to protest President Bush's March 2006 visit to India. Second, opposition from leftist parties influenced India's Iran policy. The left argued that Indian government decisions against Iran deviated from a Common Minimum Program that the left had negotiated with the Congress Party as a condition for its support. Thus, after India's September 2005 IAEA vote against Iran, the left strongly hinted that it could withdraw support for the Congress-led government (which would have led to the government's collapse) if it again voted against Iran. Ultimately, favorable last-minute international developments (related to Russia and China's also voting against Iran) made it politically easier for India's government to vote against Iran in February 2006, but it still had to remain sensitive to leftist and Muslim concerns in its broader policy toward Iran.

> *A combination of strategic considerations and domestic political reasons caused New Delhi to maintain high-level political ties with Tehran*

Thus, a combination of strategic considerations and domestic political reasons caused New Delhi to maintain high-level political ties with Tehran and to continue gas pipeline talks with Tehran in the mid-2000s. Simultaneously, however, the strong disincentive of reduced US congressional support for the US-India civilian nuclear agreement influenced India's government to align with US preferences on nuclear and defense issues related to Iran. Later, from 2010 onwards, the disincentive of incurring US sanctions influenced New Delhi to cut its oil imports from Iran. Looking ahead, the lifting of international sanctions on Iran would reduce, but may not entirely eliminate, US-India policy differences on Iran.

Arms Sales

Arms sales have been another major issue in US-India relations. In 2001, the Bush administration lifted sanctions on military interactions with India that had been imposed after its 1998 nuclear tests. It then anticipated that New Delhi would purchase a large quantity of arms from US suppliers, aiming to increase profits for US firms and tie India closer to Washington in military terms. However, New Delhi's arms imports from the United States were initially still low, valued at less than US$1 billion between 2001 and 2004. They subsequently grew to US$3 billion between 2005 and 2008 and to US$11 billion between 2009 and 2015. As a result, by then, New Delhi's arms imports converged with US expectations to a moderate-to-high extent—they stood at US$15 billion for the 2001–2015 period, only slightly below the high levels of US$20–30 billion for America's leading arms customers.[16]

India's main arms orders from the United States included the following:[17]

- Transport aircraft: six C-130J Hercules (US$1 billion) in early 2008, six additional C-130J Hercules (US$1 billion) in 2011, and ten C-17 Globemasters (US$4.7 billion) in 2011.[18]
- Maritime patrol aircraft: eight P-8 Poseidons (US$2 billion) in late 2008, and four additional P-8 Poseidons (US$1 billion) in 2013.
- Helicopters: 15 Chinook heavy-lift helicopters (US$1 billion) in 2012, 22 Apache attack helicopters (US$1.4 billion) in 2012, and 16 Sikorsky Seahawk helicopters (US$1 billion) in 2014.
- Aircraft engines: 20 GE-F404 engines (US$100 million) for India's light combat aircraft in 2002-2003, 20 additional GE-F404 engines (US$100 million) in 2007, 100 GE-F414 engines (US$800 million) in 2010, and 270 Honeywell F125 engines (US$700 million) for India's Jaguar aircraft in 2013.
- Additional Weapon Systems: 12 Raytheon Firefinder artillery radars (US$200 million) in 2002; 10 GE-LM-2500 gas turbines for Indian naval ships (US$60–100 million) in 2002–2003 (these were delivered over the next ten years, and powered three Indian frigates and India's new aircraft carrier); an amphibious ship (US$50 million) in 2006; 500 CBU-97 guided bombs (US$250 million) in 2010; 20 Harpoon antiship missiles (US$170 million) in 2010; 20 additional

Harpoon missiles (US$200 million) in 2012; and 145 howitzers (US$885 million) in 2012.

In 2011, however, New Delhi rejected US F-16 and F-18 aircraft in favor of France's Rafale for its single biggest arms order—an estimated US$15 billion deal for 126 medium multi-role combat aircraft (it should be noted that New Delhi did not finalize the Rafale order for the next three years and, in 2015, indicated that it would buy only 36 rather than 126 Rafales). Washington was particularly disappointed because, in 2010, it had supported New Delhi for a permanent seat on the UN Security Council and removed nine Indian organizations from its Entity List—initiatives that required spending much political capital within the US bureaucracy and which Washington assumed would help it secure the combat aircraft deal (Latif 2012).

New Delhi's arms import policies noted above were influenced by domestic bureaucratic and political factors. In the early and mid-2000s, India and the United States had little bureaucratic knowledge about each other's defense sales practices. New Delhi, for example, follows a two-stage competition in selecting arms suppliers, based on technical criteria (the first stage) and pricing (the second stage). In contrast, US firms emphasize the better overall value of their products based on superior technology and competitive, long-term life-cycle costs. Moreover, the United States and India have different positions on offset agreements (that is, arrangements for the arms seller to reinvest, or "offset," arms sales proceeds in the purchasing country). India tends to require offsets to be 30 percent of large contracts (and, in the mid-2010s, it introduced a related policy giving preference to arms suppliers who would manufacture items in India under the "Make in India" policy), while the United States leaves this to be negotiated by individual vendors. Both countries also have differing positions on technology transfers (India seeks these while the United States restricts them). Further, India would not accept US end-use monitoring policies. Therefore, it was only in the late 2000s—after Washington and New Delhi better understood each other's defense transfer policies and removed some barriers to defense trade by signing an end-use agreement in July 2009—that India's arms procurements from the United States increased.

Despite purchasing increasing quantities of American arms, India rejected the US F-16s and F-18s because of another domestic political factor—the politicization of arms deals. India's defense purchases attract considerable media and political attention, special parliamentary committees have often investigated allegations of defense corruption, and, for these reasons, Indian governments—at least publicly—have often insisted on following standard procurement practices (Mukherjee and Thyagraj 2012). Consequently, New Delhi followed its standard two-stage practice in selecting the medium combat aircraft and it eliminated US aircraft based on technical criteria such as their lower engine and aerodynamic performance and their older vintage (Tellis 2011).[19]

One additional domestic factor—economic constraints—also influenced India's arms procurements. Illustrating this, India's economy grew at just 4.7 percent in 2013, and this, along with a currency depreciation, reduced the funding available for defense modernization. Accordingly, only US$477 million of India's US$1.2 billion military procurement budget was available for new purchases in 2013 (Albright Stonebridge Group 2014). India therefore delayed its 2011–13 orders for howitzers, Apache and Chinook helicopters, and P-8 aircraft, and these only advanced in 2015.[20]

To summarize, India's policies on arms imports aligned with US preferences to a moderate-to-high extent, but only after gradual adjustments. Better accommodation of bureaucratic procedures on both sides accounted for the slow but increasing convergence between Indian policies and US interests on arms sales.

Bilateral Defense and Security Cooperation

While the US-India relationship in the area of arms deals improved significantly over time, the countries' bilateral defense and security cooperation has varied across issues. Since the 2000s, Washington and New Delhi discussed defense and security cooperation on four main issues—military exercises, counterterrorism, cybersecurity, and defense coproduction. New Delhi's policies on these issues converged, on average, to a low-to-moderate extent with US preferences: convergence was moderate on military exercises and low on counterterrorism, cybersecurity, and defense coproduction (though it was trending upward on some of these issues by 2015).

The United States and India held a large number of military exercises—approximately 70—from the early 2000s to 2012 (Kronstadt and Pinto 2013). Their navies have conducted up to four exercises each year—three small exercises (Habu Nag, focusing on amphibious operations; Spitting Cobra, focusing on explosive ordnance destruction; and Salvex, covering diving and salvage) and the larger Malabar exercises that include a variety of naval operations. Their armies have conducted the

While US arms sales to India increased significantly over time, the countries' bilateral defense and security cooperation on other issues has varied considerably

Yudh Abhyas exercise annually since 2004. These simulated operations such as UN peacekeeping, counterinsurgency, and counterterrorism.

Still, while both sides declare that India holds more exercises with the United States than with any other country, the depth of interaction and number of troops involved in these exercises—typically several tens in the smaller exercises and hundreds in the larger ones—were significantly less than the number (typically tens of thousands) involved in major US military exercises with its North Atlantic Treaty Organization (NATO) and Asian allies.

In the arena of counterterrorism, Washington and New Delhi set up a joint working group that has been meeting since 2000 (Olapally 2005). It discussed topics such as tackling terrorist financing, homeland security policy, border management policy, aviation security, and disaster management during a terrorist incident involving weapons of mass destruction. However, a trust deficit affected the US-India dialogue because New Delhi believed that Washington was not strongly condemning Islamabad for Pakistan-based terrorist activities against India (Curtis 2011). This somewhat eased after the 2008 Mumbai attacks, when Washington and New Delhi better coordinated their separate investigations into the attack.[21] Later, in 2010, both sides agreed on a counterterrorism cooperation initiative; in May 2011, they began a homeland security dialogue; and, subsequently, they discussed additional items such as US assistance to India in transportation security, urban policing, and law enforcement collaboration

(Fitch et al. 2013). Overall, given that the US-India dialogue expanded to cover a range of items; that US police and security agencies learned some valuable counterterrorism lessons from their investigations into and analysis of the 2008 Mumbai attacks; and that Indian authorities learned similar lessons from US best practices in the field, New Delhi's alignment with US preferences on counterterrorism is categorized as low but not negligible. It could only be classified as moderate or high if there was more substantive counterterrorism cooperation between the two sides, such as deeper intelligence sharing and joint operations against specific terrorist groups.

Similar problems undermined cooperation in the area of cybersecurity. Washington and New Delhi discussed the issue since the mid-2000s. However, a 2006 spying allegation at a cybersecurity forum, and revelations from the Edward Snowden files that the National Security Agency had tracked India, heightened Indian suspicions of US intentions (Observer Research Foundation 2014b). As a result, while both sides continued their cybersecurity dialogue in the 2010s, the depth of cooperation in this dialogue was limited.

New Delhi's policies on defense coproduction initially did not converge with US preferences either. In 2012, under a Defense Technology and Trade Initiative, Washington offered New Delhi coproduction possibilities for the Sikorsky Seahawk naval helicopter, the Javelin anti-tank missile, a 127 mm naval gun, and a delivery system for scatterable mines. US companies would provide the technology to build these weapons in India and would sell them overseas. India's government did not take up these coproduction offers and it rejected the Javelin in favor of an Israeli anti-tank missile. In mid-2015, however, under their renewed ten-year defense cooperation agreement, the two sides announced that they would discuss the coproduction of four additional systems. These were the Raven mini-unmanned aerial vehicle (which the Indian army rejected in late 2015), a surveillance module for the C-130J Hercules aircraft that support Indian Special Forces, mobile hybrid-electric power sources, and uniforms integrated with chemical and biological protection measures. Subsequently, they also explored technology transfers of an electromagnetic launch system for India's aircraft carrier and of GE-F414 engines for India's light combat aircraft. Thus, by 2015, New Delhi's policy convergence with US preferences on defense coproduction increased from negligible to low, and it could further increase to moderate or high levels should the above projects move ahead.

Strategic considerations explain why New Delhi chose to engage with Washington on the above issues—interaction with the United States had the potential of significantly enhancing India's military and security capabilities. Yet bureaucratic factors stalled the US-India dialogue. India's foreign affairs bureaucracy remained suspicious of US ties with Pakistan, leading to a trust deficit in counterterrorism. Concerning defense coproduction, Indian officials held the view that US firms wanted to capture the Indian market for the coproduced weapons rather than have them compete under India's standard defense procurement process; this influenced New Delhi's decision to not approve US coproduction overtures in the early 2010s (Business Standard 2013). This Indian thinking eased somewhat by 2015, leading to the announcement of the abovementioned four coproduction initiatives. Still, India's bureaucracy held back on signing three foundational agreements (on sharing classified information, logistics support, and geospatial cooperation) and Washington therefore hesitated to undertake more substantial defense cooperation with New Delhi. During the Indian defense minister's 2015 visit to the United States (the first by an Indian defense minister since 2008), New Delhi agreed to take a fresh look at the logistics agreement, and in early 2016 it tentatively accepted this agreement.

Nuclear Reactor Contracts

In the mid and late 2000s, when the United States and India negotiated their civilian nuclear agreement, US officials and business leaders assumed that India would award reactor contracts to US firms. They also urged New Delhi to adopt liability legislation consistent with international practices. In a September 2008 letter-of-intent, just ahead of US congressional approval for the nuclear deal, India's government committed to awarding US firms contracts for reactors generating ten thousand megawatts (MW) of electricity (worth an estimated US$50 billion). The letter also affirmed that India would adopt "an adequate nuclear liability regime." But while India's government began drafting liability legislation in 2008, it then held back on the issue while it negotiated a reprocessing pact with the United States. It eventually introduced a liability bill in parliament in March

2010, ahead of Prime Minister Singh's April visit to the United States. This bill drew upon legislation in other countries and conformed to the international Convention on Supplementary Compensation for Nuclear Damage (CSC). It held the operators of nuclear plants, rather than the suppliers of nuclear reactors, liable for any accidents. Yet the bill did not advance through the parliament. In August 2010, India adopted a different bill that held nuclear suppliers liable for damages; this appeared contrary to international norms and made it financially too risky for US firms to invest in India's nuclear sector.

> *India's liability laws held nuclear suppliers liable for damages; this made it financially too risky for US firms to invest in India's nuclear sector*

Domestic politics explain why New Delhi adopted such a liability law, resulting in a major policy divergence with the United States. In early 2010, India's government, led by the Congress Party, had reached out to the left and the right to secure their support for its initial liability bill, but they opposed it. The government therefore could not advance the bill in March 2010. The Congress Party–led coalition had 260 seats in a 540-seat parliament but a coalition partner with 19 seats had opposed nuclear reactors in its home state and was undecided on the liability bill. Further, because of poor floor management, another 30 coalition members of parliament were absent when the government introduced the bill. This reduced the ruling coalition's votes to around 210 and gave the opposition a chance to defeat the bill. India's government then withdrew the bill.

In May 2010, India's government resubmitted the bill to parliament. From June to August, the parliamentary standing committee on science and technology held several hearings on the bill. It heard testimony from government ministries, civil society experts, nuclear experts, and industrial groups. (At this time, the liability and safety issue gained more salience because of an unrelated development—a June 2010 Indian court ruling on the Bhopal disaster that reactivated domestic sentiments about holding foreign suppliers accountable for industrial accidents.) As a result of these deliberations, and after additional meetings with the BJP in August, the government accepted opposition concerns that the liability cap be raised from Rs. 500 crore (US$80 million) to Rs. 1,500 crore (US$240 million), and that nuclear suppliers be liable for accidents. It included these in its August 2010 liability legislation.

Simply put, New Delhi's August 2010 liability law was diametrically opposed to US interests. However, New Delhi did not dismiss US concerns outright—it sought to accommodate US firms through alternative mechanisms. In 2010–11, it suggested that their concerns could be resolved in individual contracts with India's government and by India's signing the CSC (which it did in October 2010, though it held back on ratifying the convention for the next five years). New Delhi then issued rules stating that suppliers would only be liable during the first five years of a reactor's operation and only up to a limit of Rs. 1,500 crore (US$240 million). While US firms did not accept this proposed solution, they did continue talks with India's government. Throughout the early 2010s the liability issue was discussed in US-India strategic talks (illustrating that both sides recognized its importance for their strategic relations); op-eds in the Indian press sometimes called for changing India's liability laws to better accommodate US and Indian business; and US firms took preparatory steps for nuclear investments in India by signing early works agreements.

Eventually, at their September 2014 meeting, Prime Minister Modi and President Obama committed to resolving the liability issue ahead of their next meeting. A US-India contact group then held three rounds of talks in New Delhi (December 16-17, 2014), Vienna (January 6-7, 2015), and London (January 21-22, 2015). In these, the Indian side suggested proposals for an enhanced insurance pool worth US$200 million and for a clarification of the liability law. The two sides announced a compromise on these items during President Obama's January 2015 visit to India (Bagchi 2015; The Hindu 2015; Ministry of External Affairs 2015). India's government then set up a Rs. 1,500 crore (US$240 million) insurance pool from which any supplier liability would be paid. It also adopted a "memorandum of law" stating that suppliers would not be liable in any nuclear accident claims and that suppliers could not be sued by Indian nuclear operators unless this was explicitly stated in their contract. And, in late 2015, the contact group discussed pricing issues for any US-supplied reactors as well as India's ratification of the CSC, which occurred in January 2016.

In sum, for six years (2008-14), New Delhi's policies did not converge with US preferences on nuclear liability and this was largely because of domestic politics. The two sides then made progress in 2015 so that India's policies converged better with US preferences, though still to a low extent. India's policy convergence with US preferences would increase to moderate if it were to finalize reactor contracts and US firms actually began reactor construction; it would increase to high if the reactors were to become operational.

The discussion above has analyzed six issues in US-India relations in some depth and assessed the extent to which India's policies converged with US interests on these issues. In the following pages, six additional cases are examined more briefly: UN peacekeeping, Indian Ocean security, Afghanistan, Pakistan, nuclear arms control, and Iraq.

UN Peacekeeping

The United States has traditionally held expectations that other nations, especially those friendly with it, should significantly contribute to UN peacekeeping operations, partly in order to reduce the financial and logistical burden of the US military presence around the world. India has found it easy to meet these expectations, aligning its own interests with those of the United States.

> *New Delhi has been a major contributor to UN peacekeeping since the 1950s and it maintained these large peacekeeping contributions in the 2000s and 2010s*

New Delhi has been a major contributor to UN peacekeeping since the 1950s and it maintained these large peacekeeping contributions in the 2000s and 2010s.

Indeed, during Prime Minister Vajpayee's visit to the United States in 2000, the two sides expressed their desire to work together to strengthen the peacekeeping component of the international security system (Embassy of India 2000). Subsequently, a joint US-India working group on peacekeeping held ten meetings between 2000 and

2013. During these years, India was one of the top three contributors to UN peacekeeping operations, deploying 8,000–10,000 peacekeepers annually (roughly similar to the contributions by the two other largest contributors, Pakistan and Bangladesh). In 2014, it contributed 8,000 personnel (7,000 troops and 900 police) to UN peacekeeping, a significant fraction of the 100,000 security personnel and 17,000 civilian police involved in 15 UN peacekeeping operations globally. In 2015, building upon a theme discussed at their 2013 joint working group meeting, the United States and India committed to enhance "peacekeeping capacity building in third countries" through "a focus on training aspects for UN peacekeepers" (The White House 2015b).

New Delhi's high UN peacekeeping contributions can be explained by domestic factors and international incentives. To begin with, because of its strong historical affinity for UN peacekeeping and for multilateral approaches to international security, domestic support for peacekeeping was firmly entrenched in New Delhi's foreign policy culture and there was, therefore, little bureaucratic or political resistance to continuing this tradition (Daniel, Taft, and Wiharta 2008; Bannerjee 2013). Moreover, two international incentives influenced New Delhi's peacekeeping policies. First, the UN's economic incentive of reimbursing peacekeeping costs made peacekeeping financially viable. Second, the implicit, but not formal, political incentive of future permanent membership on the UN Security Council sustained New Delhi's commitment to peacekeeping. The subtle influence of this incentive is reflected in a statement by an Indian commander of UN peacekeeping forces: "As a great country we have certain commitments; if we aspire to be permanent members of the UN Security Council it cannot come on a platter—we must develop a stake in strengthening the Security Council set-up and such [peacekeeping] missions help do just that" (Sorenson and Wood 2005, 202–3). Thus, key incentives influenced New Delhi to maintain its high contributions to UN peacekeeping and, by implication, align to a high extent with US objectives on this issue.

Indian Ocean Security

US officials have frequently noted that they desire India to "be a partner and net provider of security in the Indian Ocean" (Gates 2009).

New Delhi's policies have converged moderately with these US interests in three ways. First, and most generally, the Indian navy and coast guard have provided some security for (but not routine monitoring of) eight major international shipping lanes off India's coasts.

Second, since the mid-2000s, India has increased its security interactions with nearby Indian Ocean states, enabling it to play a greater security role in the region. In particular, it developed a maritime initiative with four states—Seychelles, the Maldives, Mauritius, and Sri Lanka—that included setting up radar stations, securing berthing rights for its vessels, and holding joint naval exercises (Ranasinghe 2014; The Hindu 2014). For example, India supplied a patrol boat and a Dornier patrol aircraft to Seychelles; installed coastal radar in, and leased or supplied patrol boats to, Mauritius and the Maldives; and held exercises with the Sri Lankan navy and trained Sri Lanka navy personnel. It also undertook naval exercises with, and secured berthing rights for Indian naval vessels in, Oman (Observer Research Foundation 2014a).

Third, the Indian navy undertook some significant operations in the Indian Ocean region. Two were small-scale, involving only one or two vessels. In the first, from April to September 2002, an Indian patrol vessel escorted a total of 24 US ships transiting the Straits of Malacca for the war in Afghanistan. In the second, from October 2008 onward, the Indian navy sent one to two ships to assist international antipiracy efforts in the Gulf of Aden; it extended these operations to the East Arabian Sea in 2011. By 2015, it had reportedly escorted some 3,000 ships and foiled about 40 piracy attempts in these areas. Two other operations were somewhat larger. In December 2004 and January 2005, the Indian navy quickly deployed a dozen vessels and over a thousand personnel toward tsunami relief operations in Sri Lanka, the Maldives, and Indonesia (Shukla 2005; Lancaster 2005). And, in early 2015, India evacuated 4,700 Indian nationals and 1,000 nationals of other countries from the war in Yemen. In conducting the evacuation, it drew upon three naval vessels, two civilian ships, a handful of passenger jets, and US-supplied Indian air force C-17s (three C-17 flights carried some 600 persons).

Strategic, bureaucratic, and economic factors shaped New Delhi's abovementioned policies on Indian Ocean security. Strategically, New Delhi sought to better protect sea-lanes through which its trade transited and this converged with US interests that India be a security provider in the region. Still, bureaucratic factors limited the extent to which India partnered with the United States—India's bureaucracy viewed the Indian Ocean as its sphere of influence, sought to limit the role of external powers in this region, and therefore held back from extensive partnering with the United States (Samaranayake et al. 2013; Brewster 2015). Illustrating this, India operated its abovementioned antipiracy missions independent of the US-organized Combined Maritime Forces command. Similarly, it did not formally join a US-organized Indian Ocean naval task force on terrorism. Further, economic constraints—both in terms of building up a large navy and sustaining its logistics—limited India's capacity to undertake large-scale operations over a prolonged time period in the Indian Ocean region.

Afghanistan

New Delhi's policies on the war in Afghanistan converged moderately with US state-building objectives for the country but with some nuances. India disbursed about US$800 million in economic and humanitarian assistance to Afghanistan by 2015 (typically in annual installments of US$50–100 million), out of a total aid pledge of US$2 billion. This was moderate in magnitude compared to the higher commitments of US$3–5 billion made by six larger donors—the United Kingdom (UK), Japan, the European Union (EU), the World Bank, the Asian Development Bank, and Germany. New Delhi's assistance funded social and human development projects, such as food assistance to school children and the building of schools; construction of the Afghan parliament building (completed in 2015); infrastructure projects such as the Salma hydroelectric dam (to be completed in 2016); and a 200 kilometer (km) road from the Kandahar-Herat highway to the Iranian border that goes on to the Iranian port of Chabahar, and enables India to transport heavy supplies to Afghanistan (Price 2013; Mullen 2016).

New Delhi's economic assistance furthered US and international state-building objectives in Afghanistan but had a mixed overall impact because of Pakistan's reaction. Islamabad's security agencies believed that Pakistan was being flanked by a hostile India and an India-leaning Afghanistan. They had links with the Taliban-affiliated

Haqqani network, and the Taliban insurgency undermined state-building in Afghanistan (Reidel 2013; Darymple 2013).[22] Washington and New Delhi only better recognized this dynamic (that is, a correlation between Indian engagement in Afghanistan and Pakistani support for the Taliban) in the late 2000s, after which New Delhi did not expand its security presence in Afghanistan.[23] Accordingly, while Indian paramilitary units guarded Indian diplomatic posts and some infrastructure projects, New Delhi did not deploy regular military forces to Afghanistan. Also, in 2014, it held back on an Afghan government request for Indian weapons (in late 2015, however, it transferred four of its aging Russian-made Mi-25 attack helicopters to Afghanistan). Overall, strategic interests influenced New Delhi to develop a strategic partnership with Afghanistan that included assisting state-building in Afghanistan, but Pakistan's reaction to these efforts negatively impacted the overall war in Afghanistan.

Pakistan
New Delhi's policies on Pakistan aligned with US objectives in a fluctuating manner: alignment was low in the early 2000s, moderate from 2004 to 2007, low-to-moderate from 2008 to mid-2015, and trending toward moderate by early 2016. This fluctuation, of course, reflected the ups and downs in the India-Pakistan relationship itself. From a US perspective, the ideal Indian policy toward Pakistan would be to advance the India-Pakistan peace process, reduce Pakistan's security concerns about India, and thereby further US interests in Afghanistan and Pakistan. According to this logic, India-Pakistan normalization could make Pakistan less likely to support the Taliban in Afghanistan; could reduce the risks of a political and military crisis escalating into a war involving the possible use of nuclear weapons; could enable Pakistan to adopt safer nuclear security practices during peacetime; and could help Islamabad focus more on development, which would reduce the risks of state-failure in Pakistan and of extremists taking control of Pakistan's tribal areas (US Department of State 2013; Markey 2013).

In the early 2000s, New Delhi's policies did not converge with these US objectives because India and Pakistan were close to war. From December 2001 to mid-2002, New Delhi mobilized several hundred thousand troops for a possible military attack against Pakistan in response to years of Pakistan-linked militant attacks in Kashmir and an especially provocative December 2001 attack on India's parliament. From 2004 to 2007, however, New Delhi's policies converged moderately with US objectives, as Pakistan and India began back-channel peace talks and a formal "composite dialogue." They undertook limited confidence-building measures and enhanced people-to-people contacts through bus and train services. India-Pakistan trade also increased from US$344 million in 2003–2004 to nearly US$2 billion in 2007–08, though it remained at US$2–2.5 billion per year until the early 2010s, which was less than 1 percent of India's overall trade (Kugelman and Hathaway 2013). The dialogue then slowed due to a political transition in Pakistan and halted after the November 2008 Mumbai terrorist attacks (Cohen, Chari, and Cheema 2007; Coll 2009; International Crisis Group 2012).

> *In the absence of a sustained peace process, New Delhi's policies on Pakistan converged with US objectives of India-Pakistan normalization only to a low-to-moderate extent*

Subsequently, in the absence of a sustained peace process, New Delhi's policies on Pakistan converged with US objectives only to a low-to-moderate extent. In 2009, statements by Indian defense officials about the feasibility of military strikes against Pakistan exacerbated India-Pakistan tensions. New Delhi and Islamabad resumed their composite dialogue in July 2011 but the dialogue halted again in early 2013 after cross-border skirmishes killed Indian soldiers. Thereafter, while Indian and Pakistani diplomats met occasionally, India suspended high-level talks in August 2014 and firings across the line of control escalated—occurring during 21 percent of the days in 2013, 20 percent of the days in 2014, and 23 percent of the days in early 2015 (compared to 7 percent of the days in 2011 and 10 percent in 2012; Thompson 2015). In late 2015, New Delhi and Islamabad sought to resume the peace process and New Delhi's policy alignment with US objectives then trended upward toward moderate levels.[24]

Strategic considerations, external spoilers, and domestic factors have influenced New Delhi's policies on Pakistan. On strategic grounds, New Delhi felt it could not advance the peace process until it was reasonably assured that Pakistan's security establishment ended its support for militants targeting India.[25] It also sought concrete measures from Pakistan in prosecuting the perpetrators of the Mumbai terrorist attacks (in the early 2010s, Pakistan's government had commenced but not completed trial proceedings against seven persons accused in the attacks). Pakistan's security agencies, and their support for militants, thus became prominent spoilers of the India-Pakistan peace process. In the arena of domestic politics, media and political pressure to take a hard line on Pakistan, especially after militant attacks and provocative incidents, made it difficult for India's government to advance peace talks. For example, in the early 2010s, the Indian media excessively covered incidents such as the "beheading" of an Indian soldier by Pakistani troops and the killing of an Indian prisoner in Pakistan, creating significant obstacles to reconciliation (Times of India 2013a; Times of India 2013b). India's right-wing opposition parties took a similar line and often called for India's government to suspend peace talks with Pakistan (Indian Express 2013). When the right-wing came to power in mid-2014, however, it adopted a more nuanced position—while it held back on the peace process until mid-2015, it sought to resume the dialogue with Pakistan in late 2015.

Nuclear Arms Control

In its 1998–99 nuclear talks with India, the Clinton administration sought Indian restraints on nuclear testing, fissile material production, and missile expansion (Talbott 2004). Over the next decade, New Delhi's policies converged with these US objectives only to a low extent.

While New Delhi maintained a nuclear testing moratorium after its 1998 nuclear tests, it did not legally codify this and did not sign the Comprehensive Nuclear-Test-Ban Treaty. Moreover, it did not halt fissile material production, though its main military-related reactor only produced plutonium sufficient for five weapons per year. Finally, India advanced its missile program—in the 2000s and early 2010s, it typically tested one new missile every three years. Thus, New Delhi's nuclear weapons policies aligned with US objectives to a moderate level on nuclear test restraints, to a low level on fissile material restraints, and to a negligible level on missile restraints; on the average, therefore, they converged with US preferences to a low level.

Strategic considerations and domestic factors prevented India from undertaking significant nuclear weapon restraints. Strategically, New Delhi sought to build up its nuclear capabilities versus China and Pakistan. Domestically, the Department of Atomic Energy and the Defense Research and Development Organization each had dedicated programs to develop an array of warheads and missiles and this provided the bureaucratic push for these programs. Politically, Indian governments found it prudent to support these—popular—programs. As a result, while maintaining nuclear test restraints, New Delhi did not curb its missile program and fissile material production.

Iraq

On the war in Iraq, the policy alignment between India and the United States was negligible, though India did not take an anti-US position on the issue. In 2003, after initial major combat operations concluded with the ouster of Saddam Hussein's regime, the Bush administration requested India to send a battalion of 17,000 troops for noncombat stabilization operations in the Kurdish regions of Iraq. President Bush raised the issue with Deputy Prime Minister L. K. Advani during his June 2003 visit to Washington; senior US officials and the Pentagon held detailed discussions with Indian officials on the politics and logistics of the issue; India's government sent emissaries to Iraq and neighboring countries to assess the situation; and the Indian military started planning for possible deployments. India's government thus actively considered the US request but ultimately declined it in July 2003 (R. Chaudhuri 2014). Its official reason was the absence of a UN mandate: "were there to be an explicit UN mandate for the purpose, the Government of India could consider the deployment of our troops in Iraq" (Economic Times 2013). However, New Delhi did not take an anti-US position. Instead, India's national security advisor called his US counterpart to explain India's decision before publicly announcing it. In the same vein, India's government only mildly condemned the US intervention in Iraq (though Indian civil society and Indian opposition parties were more critical).

New Delhi then made small-scale efforts to assist Iraq's reconstruction. Thus, in 2003–2004, it committed US$10 million to the

International Reconstruction Fund Facility for Iraq (this was just a small fraction of the US$1.8 billion total international contributions to the fund at the time) and another US$20 million in bilateral aid to Iraq.

New Delhi's decision to not send troops to Iraq was largely due to domestic considerations. Some analysts and BJP leaders favored Indian troop deployments in Iraq, making the case that this would strengthen India's ties with the United States, and that India could avail itself of US incentives, though these were somewhat unclear.[26] Yet the domestic resistance was much greater—not only in the media and from opposition parties but also from some of the BJP's coalition partners. The opposing arguments are best reflected in a statement by two former prime ministers, V. P. Singh and Inder Gujral. They wrote: "We believe irreparable damage will be done to India's reputation and good name, if Indian troops were sent to prop up the occupation of Iraq," and that, "[A]bove all, it will be unwise and unfair to our army to send them on a mission to risk their lives where no national interest is at stake" (Kifner 2003). Against this backdrop of domestic opposition, and the absence of a UN mandate through which Indian governments had historically sent troops to overseas conflicts, Prime Minister Vajpayee decided against sending Indian troops to Iraq. At a meeting of the Cabinet Committee on Security, after a debate between opponents and proponents of sending troops to Iraq, a proponent noted that it was decided that India would join the US coalition; Vajpayee responded, "Who has decided?" and this ended the committee discussion (Panagariya 2012).

New Delhi maintained its risk-averse policy—it made small contributions toward democratization and stabilization efforts but abstained from military contributions in the Iraq war

It should be noted that, while New Delhi's policy alignment with US preferences on the war in Iraq was marginal, it was still greater than the "negative alignment" position of some West European US allies. These countries "soft balanced" against the Bush administration's position and sought to rally international diplomatic support to prevent the war. Later, in the mid and late 2000s, New Delhi maintained its risk-averse policy—it made small contributions toward democratization and stabilization efforts but abstained from military contributions in Iraq. It similarly refrained from military participation in the US-led coalition against the Islamic State in Iraq and Syria (ISIS) in the mid-2010s.

Analyzing the Cases

Overall Trends: Moderate, Uneven, and Slow Policy Convergence

When analyzing the alignment between New Delhi's policies and US strategic interests, five trends emerge. First, across the twelve cases, New Delhi's policies aligned with US objectives to a moderate extent, on the average: they aligned to a high extent in two cases; to a moderate-to-high extent in one case; to a low-to-moderate or moderate extent in six cases; and to a low or negligible extent in three cases. Thus, New Delhi's policy alignment with US objectives was, in quantitative terms, halfway between the optimist expectation and the skeptical perspective.[27]

Second, in many cases, greater convergence between New Delhi's policies and US objectives occurred slowly, over a period of years rather than months. For instance, it took five years for convergence to reach high levels on nonproliferation export controls; almost a decade to reach moderate-to-high levels on arms sales; and six years to move from negligible to low levels on nuclear deals for US firms. To be sure, this observation does not apply to all cases. In some time-sensitive cases such as disaster relief, India acted quickly—it undertook rescue operations within hours or days in response to the Asian tsunami, the Nepal earthquake, and the war in Yemen—but, in many other cases, its policies were slow to converge with US objectives.

Third, in no case did New Delhi actively oppose and seek to undermine US policies. This stands in contrast to instances where some

> *In no case did New Delhi actively oppose and seek to undermine US policies; this stands in contrast to instances where some US partners and allies directly opposed and worked against US objectives*

US partners and allies directly opposed and worked against US objectives—for example, by diplomatically opposing and seeking to avert
the 2003 Iraq war (France and Germany); politically opposing and
lobbying Congress against a nuclear agreement with Iran (Israel);
financing the propagation of extremist Wahabi ideology in some
countries (Saudi Arabia); or supporting the Taliban who fought US
and NATO troops in Afghanistan (Pakistan).

Fourth, contrary to the skepticism of the early 2010s, New Delhi's policy convergence with US objectives did not decrease under the
Obama administration when compared to the Bush administration.
Instead, in almost all cases, New Delhi's policies converged with US
objectives just as well or even to a greater extent (especially in the
cases of arms sales and export controls) under the Obama administration when compared to the Bush administration. Also, New Delhi's
policy convergence with US objectives did slightly increase under the
BJP government since mid-2014. To be sure, this was not because of
the ideological differences between the BJP and the Congress Party
but, rather, because policy paralysis had affected the last two years of
the Congress-led government's term.[28]

Fifth, the type of issue—bilateral, regional, or international security—did not influence how well New Delhi's policies aligned with
US objectives. On the five international security cases, New Delhi's
alignment with US objectives varied considerably, and was, on the
average, moderate: it was high on two cases (UN peacekeeping and
export controls), moderate on Iran, low on nuclear arms control, and
negligible on Iraq. On the three bilateral cases, New Delhi's alignment with US objectives was again, on the average, moderate: it was
moderate-to-high on arms sales; low-to-moderate on bilateral defense
cooperation; and low but trending upward on nuclear rewards for US
firms. And on the four regional cases, New Delhi's alignment with
US objectives reached low-to-moderate or moderate levels but with
considerable fluctuations at different points in time.

The Principal Factors

A mix of strategic considerations, domestic factors, incentives and
disincentives, and case-specific factors explain the extent to which
India's policies aligned with US objectives. Three observations in this
regard are particularly important. First, in cases where US objectives

advanced India's strategic interests, New Delhi's policies should have converged to a high extent with the US objective—however the actual convergence was only moderate or low-to-moderate in most cases, generally because of *domestic obstacles*. Second, in cases where US objectives did not advance India's strategic interests, New Delhi's policies should have converged to a low or negligible extent with the US objective—however they still converged to a moderate or high extent in three of five relevant cases, because of *incentives and disincentives*. Third, *other factors*, such as external spoilers and UN resolutions, also influenced New Delhi's policies in some cases. These observations can be clarified by testing two hypotheses.

Strategic Interests and Domestic Constraints

Purely strategic power-based and interest-based explanations would predict that India's policies would converge well with US objectives when the US objective advanced India's strategic interests (as defined previously in this study). Accordingly, Hypothesis 1 (H1) can be formulated as follows:

> H1: *India's policies converge at least moderately with US objectives when the US objective advances India's strategic interests.*

Hypothesis 1 can be tested on seven cases—those of nuclear reactor contracts, arms sales, defense and security cooperation, Indian Ocean security, China, Afghanistan, and Pakistan. In each of these cases, the US objective would advance India's strategic interests. Thus, US nuclear reactor sales to India would boost India's energy sector and increase its economic strength; US arms transfers would strengthen India's military capabilities; US defense and security cooperation would enhance India's capabilities in areas ranging from joint military operations to arms production to counterterrorism; US preferences that India be an Indian Ocean security provider would advance India's interests in protecting its maritime trade routes; US preferences that India balance China would advance India's strategic interests in building up its military capabilities and external partnerships to hedge against any deterioration in Sino-Indian ties; US objectives for state-building in Afghanistan would advance India's interests in a stable Afghanistan; and US preferences for India-Pakistan peace would dovetail with India's strategic interests in reducing the security threat from Pakistan through the normalization of ties.

Ultimately, six of the seven cases—all except the case of nuclear reactor contracts—do support H1. At the same time, India's policies in these cases converged with US objectives to a moderate extent, rather than to the high extent that the maximum realization of the hypothesis would entail. *Domestic factors* account for the discrepancy between the observed results and ideal-type outcomes of maximum convergence in many of these cases. (The manner in which these factors impacted India's alignment behavior are not unique to the US-India relationship—domestic politics often impede international balancing and policy convergence between allies; see Schweller 2004, von Hlatsky 2013).

> *Domestic economic constraints prevented India from purchasing greater quantities of US arms, from more substantially modernizing its military forces to balance China, and from acquiring greater naval capabilities to play a larger role in Indian Ocean security*

In particular, domestic economic constraints prevented India from purchasing greater quantities of US arms, from more substantially modernizing its military forces to balance China, and from acquiring greater naval capabilities to play a larger role in Indian Ocean security. Domestic political and bureaucratic factors also influenced these and additional cases. As noted in this study, leftist opposition in the mid-2000s prevented India from generating greater defense cooperation with the United States while bureaucratic barriers in India's arms procurement process affected some US arms deals with India. Likewise, the Indian bureaucracy's preference for maintaining "strategic autonomy" held back New Delhi from strongly aligning with Washington in balancing China, from formally joining US-led Indian Ocean antipiracy initiatives, and from deeper bilateral defense and security cooperation. Domestic political obstacles were also a factor holding back the India-Pakistan peace process in the early 2010s.

The seventh case—that of nuclear reactor contracts—does not support the hypothesis, and the explanation lies entirely in domestic politics. While aligning with US preferences and importing US nuclear reactors would have boosted India's energy capacity and advanced its economic interests, legislative politics prevented India from adopting liability laws friendly to US nuclear investors.

The Influence of Incentives and Disincentives

The converse of H1, Hypothesis 2 (H2), may be stated as follows:

> *India's policies do not converge at least moderately with US objectives when the US objective does not advance India's strategic interests.*

Hypothesis 2 predicts that India's policies converge only marginally with US objectives when the US objective does not directly advance India's strategic interests. This can be tested on five cases—nuclear arms control, Iran, Iraq, export controls, and UN peacekeeping. India's strategic interests would be set back if it weakened ties with Iran and if it accepted nuclear arms control restraints (especially when China and Pakistan were enlarging their nuclear forces). Also, while India's sending troops to Iraq, adopting stronger export controls, and contributing to UN peacekeeping did not hurt its strategic interests, they did not directly advance them either.

Ultimately, only two cases (nuclear arms control and Iraq) support Hypothesis 2, while the other three cases (Iran, export controls, and UN peacekeeping) do not. A variety of *incentives and disincentives* explain this difference between the hypothesized and observed outcomes in these three cases. In all these cases, New Delhi faced a significant disincentive if it did not adopt policies converging with US objectives. Thus, on two cases, export controls and Iran, New Delhi faced the disincentive of reduced US congressional support for the nuclear deal if it did not align with US objectives by strengthening export controls, voting against Iran at the IAEA, and curbing defense talks with Iran. Conversely, it had a major incentive—securing the civilian nuclear agreement—to adopt preferred US policies. In the third case, UN peacekeeping, India faced the implied (though not explicit) disincentive of reduced international support for its membership on the UN Security Council if it scaled back its UN peacekeeping efforts. Conversely, it had a strong implied incentive—better international support for its Security Council bid—to maintain its high peacekeeping contributions.

Disincentives also partly influenced the fourth case, nuclear arms control. Here, India faced a significant disincentive—of US sanctions and the rupture of the civilian nuclear agreement—if it conducted nuclear tests; this contributed to its nuclear test moratorium and its resulting convergence with this US preference on nuclear arms control. Significantly, it faced no disincentive if it expanded its fissile material production and missile program. In the fifth case, Iraq, an incentive was presented (the United States offered to financially compensate India's government for troop deployments and to help it secure reconstruction contracts in Iraq) and this could have potentially—under different circumstances—induced New Delhi to send troops to Iraq. Ultimately, this incentive was not sufficiently influential because it was outweighed by three other factors: the absence of Indian strategic interests, the domestic unpopularity of the war in Iraq, and the absence of a UN resolution.

A sixth example involving incentives, though outside this sample for H2, had a similar result. In 2010, the Obama administration's incentive of supporting New Delhi for a permanent seat on the UN Security Council did not persuade New Delhi to award a medium combat aircraft deal to US firms. This incentive was outweighed by domestic political factors that prevented India's government from giving US firms any special preference in the combat aircraft deal. Overall, then, incentives and disincentives influenced New Delhi's policies in three cases (two of these were directly or implicitly linked to the nuclear deal); disincentives partly influenced New Delhi's policy in a fourth case; and incentives did not influence New Delhi's policy in a fifth and sixth case.

Other Factors: External Spoilers, UN Resolutions

Two other factors influenced some of the cases: external spoilers, who reduced New Delhi's policy convergence with US objectives, and UN resolutions, which facilitated slightly greater Indian policy convergence with US objectives. Pakistan-based militants and Pakistan's security establishment played a prominent spoiler role in two cases, namely those of Pakistan and Afghanistan. First, militant attacks against India significantly disrupted the India-Pakistan peace process.

Second, Islamabad's support for the Afghan Taliban negated the potentially greater impact that Indian (and broader international) economic assistance could have had on state-building in Afghanistan.

UN resolutions also influenced some of the cases. In three cases, New Delhi better supported (or indicated that it would better support) the US preference when there was a UN resolution or UN backing on the issue. First, on export controls, UN Security Council Resolution 1540 enabled India's government to convince leftist parties to accept India adhering to the MTCR and NSG as part of the civilian nuclear agreement. Second, on Iran, India accepted US legislation on the civilian nuclear agreement when the language in such legislation was changed to seek Indian action as per UN resolutions—rather than as per US policy—on Iran. Third, UN resolutions on various peacekeeping missions facilitated Indian troop contributions to these missions.

Further, in two instances, the absence of a UN resolution hurt New Delhi's support for US policies. In the nonproliferation control issue of PSI, the absence of a UN resolution gave leftist parties stronger grounds to oppose India's formal participation in PSI. And, on the war in Iraq, India's government cited the absence of a UN resolution as a major reason for not sending troops to Iraq.

Finally, one example where a UN resolution did not increase India's convergence with a preferred US policy position should be noted: the case of piracy in the Indian Ocean. In this case, a 2008 UN Security Council resolution established a counterpiracy task force but, because of the US sponsorship of the task force and Pakistan's participation in it, India did not formally join the task force. As a compromise, it still sent one or two naval vessels for anti-piracy patrols (Brewster 2014, 175). Thus, UN resolutions have generally, but not always, helped New Delhi better align its policies with US preferences and the absence of a UN resolution has, in some cases, made it harder for Indian governments to align their policies with US positions.

The absence of a UN resolution has, in some cases, made it harder for Indian governments to align their policies with US positions

Additional Cases and Factors

This study has noted that New Delhi's policies on twelve bilateral, regional, and international security issues aligned, on the average, moderately with US objectives. A mix of strategic considerations, domestic variables, incentives and disincentives, and case-specific factors explain the uneven pattern of alignment across the cases. Further research would be necessary to test how well these findings apply to additional cases. But a few preliminary observations are possible here.

In some additional cases, unique case-specific factors may be influential. For example, in the Middle East, one relevant factor is India's population security concerns (Jaishankar 2014). These concerns, related to the safety of Indian nationals working in the region, held back Indian governments from aligning with the United States in military campaigns in the region.

Furthermore, New Delhi's voting behavior in the United Nations suggests a lower level of convergence with US preferences than in some of the issues examined in this study. For example, from 2009 to 2014, during annual UN General Assembly votes on about 80 issues (these exclude issues voted upon by consensus), New Delhi voted with the United States on just 25–35 percent of the issues, while America's Asian and European allies voted with it on over 70 percent of the issues.[29] Similarly, on issues such as the responsibility to protect and international intervention, New Delhi's approach converges more with that of the nonaligned countries and with that of Brazil, Russia, China, and South Africa (the nations other than India included as "BRICS") than with that of the United States (Sidhu, Mehta, and Jones 2013). On some of these issues, however, New Delhi's policies are similar to that of a key US ally, Germany. Germany's reluctant acquiescence to US-led sanctions on Russia was similar to India's reluctant acceptance of US-led sanctions on Iran; also, Germany, like India, Brazil, China, and Russia, abstained from the US-led 2011 UN Security Council resolution on Libya (Kundnani 2015). A detailed examination of these and additional cases would offer a firmer basis for more widely generalizing the findings from this study.

Looking Ahead

The Bush administration had high expectations for strategic relations with India during its term in office; it expected strong policy convergence with India and tried to work toward it. Eventually, however, over the course of the Bush and Obama administrations, New Delhi's policies converged, on the average, only moderately with US objectives. Hence, the US-India partnership did not live up to its initially high expectations in terms of building strong policy alignment and advancing US interests across a range of issues. At the same time, however, some cases do support optimistic views about US strategic relations with India. For example, India's arms imports from the US increased considerably by the 2010s. Also, in a case where the United States and India had diverging strategic interests—Iran—New Delhi's policies still converged moderately with Washington's preferences.

Looking ahead, with Prime Minister Modi having assumed office in 2014 and a new president arriving in the White House in 2017, the United States and India are moving toward a new phase in their relations. Will India's foreign policy alignment with the United States substantially improve in this new phase? And, even if it improves, would it backslide subsequently if a different government assumes office after India's 2019 elections? Here, the indications are mixed.

On the one hand, two factors that previously prevented greater US-India policy convergence have changed, allowing for better convergence in the future. First, because the BJP attained a parliamentary majority in the 2014 elections, domestic legislative obstacles would not excessively constrain it from pursuing pro-US policies. Second, India's bureaucracy may be less tethered to nonalignment. On this point, some analysts note that Indian political culture still tilts toward, and its foreign policy elites prefer, some form of nonalignment (Pant and Super 2015). Others, however, note that India has started moving away from nonalignment and, although "India's shift away from nonalignment remains incomplete," they expect that "continued geopolitical changes around the world, the importance of economics, and China's rise" could facilitate a structural realignment between the United States and India (Council on Foreign Relations 2015b, 4).

Partly influenced by the above changes, New Delhi's policies on some issues have aligned better with US objectives since the mid-2010s.

For instance, while leftist resistance in the mid-2000s had prevented Japan's routine inclusion in US-India naval exercises, Japan began regularly participating in these exercises since 2014. In another example, Indian diplomatic statements on the South China Sea have been closer to the US and Southeast Asian position, rather than the Chinese position, and affirmed the freedom of navigation and respect for territorial integrity in the region.

On the other hand, the above points should not imply that the BJP government's foreign policy will converge strongly with US objectives—four examples illustrate this.

First, despite its parliamentary majority, the BJP government did not amend India's nuclear liability laws as per US preferences; instead, it opted for non-legislative solutions to the liability issue.

Second, in 2014–15, Indian bureaucratic resistance to signing three foundational agreements—on sharing classified information, logistics, and geospatial cooperation—held back deeper bilateral defense cooperation with the United States.

Third, India and the United States may still have somewhat diverging positions on Iran and on the Middle East.

Fourth, even as it consolidates ties with the United States, New Delhi may well pursue "multi-alignment" and maintain strong ties with Russia. Reflecting this, New Delhi and Moscow held annual high-level summits in the 2000s and 2010s. Also, India sought and gained admission into the Shanghai Cooperation Organization that includes Russia, the former Soviet Central Asian republics, and China. Further, India partnered with Russia, rather than with the United States or West European countries, in seeking to develop a fifth generation combat aircraft (however, this project had not advanced by 2015 because of unresolved design and cost issues with the aircraft). And, during Prime Minister Modi's December 2015 visit to Russia, the two sides agreed to major projects involving the construction of Russian reactors and the manufacture of Russian Kamov-226 helicopters in India.

The above examples suggest that, barring a significant strategic shock that strongly aligns the United States and India against a major external threat, the overall conclusions of this study are likely to hold for the foreseeable future. Sometimes differing strategic interests, along with domestic political and economic obstacles, still prevent

New Delhi from firmly aligning its foreign policy with US objectives. US policymakers could thus moderate their expectations about strategic relations with India. They could certainly consider India to be a friendly democracy and an important strategic partner but should not expect it to become a military ally or a tightly aligned strategic partner. They should anticipate that New Delhi's policies on key strategic issues are unlikely, in the majority of cases, to converge with US objectives at the high level typical of strongest partners. Instead, they are likely to converge at moderate levels typical of normal strategic partners.

Endnotes

1. For early optimist views, see Blackwill 2005, Rice 2006, and Burns 2007. For more diverse perspectives in the 2010s, see Perkovich 2010, Smith 2014, Goel 2014, Twinning 2014, Lavoy and White 2015, and Boggs and Burns 2015.

2. This study discusses India's "alignment" with the United States on strategic issues, which is distinct from a formal "alliance"; on this distinction, see Wilkins 2012. Some authors note that the US-India strategic partnership is closer to an "entente," which falls between an ad hoc coalition and a formal alliance; see Hagerty 2006.

3. As Secretary of State Condoleezza Rice subsequently wrote, the Bush administration engaged India to "unlock a wide range of possible areas of cooperation with a country that was an emerging power"; that strategic "cooperation with another emerging power in Asia, especially a democratic one, was a welcome development"; and that defense trade with India "was an exciting prospect for the [US] defense industry." Rice 2011, 437.

4. In 2009–10, the Obama administration had rhetorically noted that the "G-2," comprising the United States and China, would be crucial in shaping international affairs. India's foreign policy community misperceived these remarks to imply that the administration was relegating India to a lower status than China. Relatedly, the Obama administration mentioned that China would play a key role in "South Asia"—this referred to Afghanistan, but India's political establishment misinterpreted this term to refer to India and Pakistan and it strongly opposed the suggestion of a Chinese role in the subcontinent. For a related discussion, see Shukla 2014.

5. Analysts and retired government officials also favored new versions of nonalignment, such as "Nonalignment 2.0"—see Center for Policy Research 2012.

6. Sibal, a former foreign secretary, noted that "India remains partially tethered to the underlying strategic logic of non-alignment"; in this context, "the 'strategic

partnership' meme in Indian foreign relations is [useful in] that it allows a nation that has not entirely shed its non-aligned roots to experiment with comprehensive diplomatic engagement" with another state without entering into a formal alliance.

7. Although India had a sizeable surface fleet, its force of 12 conventional submarines was declining at that time. While it ordered 6 new French Scorpene submarines to be delivered around 2018–20, these would be insufficient to fully replace the 12 Kilo and Type-109 submarines that are scheduled for retirement by the late 2010s.

8. The prior year, in their joint prime ministerial statement, reflecting a position similar to the US stance on maritime security, the two sides had "affirmed their shared commitment to maritime security, freedom of navigation and overflight, civil aviation safety, unimpeded lawful commerce, and peaceful settlement of disputes in accordance with international law" (Ministry of External Affairs 2014).

9. New Delhi affirmed its commitment to these issues at the 2013 and 2014 East Asia Summits, at the 2014 ASEAN Regional Forum meeting, and in India-US statements in September 2014 and January 2015.

10. In 2014, India's trade with China was US$70 billion, comprising US$55 billion in imports and US$15 billion in exports. In percentage terms, India's largest trading partners in the early and mid-2010s were oil-exporting countries (approximately 30 percent), the European Union (around 12 percent), China (9–10 percent, or 11–12 percent including Hong Kong), and the United States (7–8 percent).

11. The heads-of-government visits were undertaken by Prime Minister Vajpayee (2003), Premier Wen Jiabao (2005 and 2010), President Hu Jintao (2006), Prime Minister Manmohan Singh (2008 and 2013), Premier Li Keqiang (2013), and Prime Minister Modi (2015). The China-India Strategic Dialogues began in the late 2000s, with the sixth dialogue held in 2014, while the China-India Strategic Economic Dialogues took place in 2011, 2012, and 2014.

12. The United States removed from its "Entity List" three organizations under India's Defense Research and Development Organization, four subordinates of the Indian Space and Research Organization, and Bharat Dynamics Limited (which makes ballistic missiles). The "Entity List" is a list of entities, organizations, and individuals who are generally denied the transfer of industrial technologies which may be used in nuclear and missile programs.

13. In 2012, New Delhi held outreach meetings with the MTCR on January 30, the NSG on March 1, the Wassenaar Arrangement on March 21, and the Australia Group in May. In March 2013, it added MTCR-relevant items to its export control list. Eventually, however, while some of the regimes—particularly the MTCR and Australia Group—were willing to consider India's membership, NSG members were unwilling until they themselves defined the terms for admitting new members. As a result, in 2013–15, even though the United States acknowledged that India had met the requirements for joining the NSG, New Delhi had not been admitted to this group nor to the other export control regimes.

14. In September 2006, India's foreign secretary informed US officials that India would not be able to endorse PSI until the civilian nuclear agreement was complete. In an April 2007 meeting, US Assistant Secretary Boucher urged New Delhi to endorse the PSI statement of principles, adding that the information Washington had provided New Delhi the previous year should satisfy its concerns. US Embassy 2007.

15. Reflecting the state of India-Iran diplomacy in the early 2010s, Indian foreign secretaries visited Iran in February 2010 and July 2011, the speaker of India's parliament visited Iran in November 2011, and Iran's foreign minister visited India in May 2012. Also, India's external affairs minister visited Tehran for the May 2010 G-15 summit while Prime Minister Singh attended the August 2012 nonaligned summit in Tehran. At these multilateral meetings, New Delhi did not support Tehran's anti-US position; for example, at the 2012 nonaligned meeting, it did not back excessively anti-US proposals sponsored by Iran and instead sought to moderate these.

16. From 2001 to 2015, US arms export orders to its Asia-Pacific allies (Australia, Japan, and South Korea) and to major Middle East clients (Israel, Qatar, and the UAE) were valued at US$20 billion to US$30 billion each, while those with Saudi Arabia were over US$50 billion. Also, in this period, the United States ranked as India's second-largest arms supplier. India's arms orders from the United States were somewhat below its arms orders from Russia (US$25–30 billion when including a US$12 billion deal for 270 Su-30 aircraft); they were comparable to those from France (about US$15 billion when including 36 Rafale aircraft [whose price had risen to US$8 billion by 2015], 6 Scorpene submarines [US$4 billion], Mirage-2000 aircraft upgrades [US$2 billion], and Mirage-2000 air-to-air missiles [US$1.2 billion]); and greater than those from Israel (approximately US$10 billion).

17. Arms orders are indicated in the year that India selected US suppliers for the order; the actual order was sometimes finalized one to three years later and payments and deliveries occurred over a period of years after the order was finalized.

18. New Delhi also considered buying three additional C-17s in 2015 but the status of this purchase remains unclear since Boeing had ended production of the aircraft by then and did not have fresh inventories to sell to India.

19. Other reasons may also have influenced the decision. As previously noted, India's foreign policy establishment was suspicious of the Obama administration's engagement with China: "The MMRCA [medium multi role combat aircraft] bidding took place when the so-called G-2 policy was in full swing between the Obama administration and Beijing." This, along with technical criteria for a two-engine aircraft, "ensured that there was no political interference from the pro-U.S. prime minister Manmohan Singh in favor of the U.S. bids." P. Chaudhuri 2014.

20. The howitzer contract advanced in 2015 after the supplier, a US subsidiary of British Aerospace, committed to investing US$200 million for an assembly integration and test facility in partnership with an Indian company. Also, the

Apache and Chinook helicopter deal was finally approved by India's Defence Acquisition Council in August 2014, by the finance wing of the Ministry of Defence in April 2015, and by the Cabinet Committee on Security in September 2015, ahead of Prime Minister Modi's visit to the United States. And the order for four P-8 aircraft was approved by the Defence Acquisition Council in July 2015. In another case, the 2011 contract for 10 C-17s gave India the option to purchase six additional C-17s but lack of funding kept India from exercising this clause; in 2015, after the C-17 demonstrated its utility in Yemen and Nepal, the Indian Air Force asked the government to approve the purchase of an additional three C-17s.

21. In investigating the Mumbai attacks, the Federal Bureau of Investigation (FBI) had greater access to intelligence from India, as well as the opportunity to interview 70 individuals including the sole surviving attacker, while US technical assistance helped India develop leads in its investigation and understand the command and control of the operation. Subsequently, in October 2009, US authorities arrested the Pakistan-born US citizen David Headley for conspiring in the Mumbai attacks and prosecuted him in a US court. New Delhi was still concerned that Indian authorities were not given direct access to Headley for nine months after his arrest and that Washington did not seek the prosecution of Pakistani intelligence officers named by Headley for their involvement in the Mumbai attacks. See Curtis 2011.

22. It should be clarified that rivalry with India was a major, but not the only, reason behind Islamabad's support for the Taliban; it is analytically difficult to ascertain whether Islamabad would not have supported the Taliban if India had not been involved in Afghanistan. On this point, see Nadir 2014.

23. Reflecting this point, analysts noted that "India's [security] role in Afghanistan to date has been limited, and intentionally so, because Washington and Delhi and Kabul and other key capitals have recognized the potential for any larger Indian role to have undesirable effects." See O'Hanlon 2013. See also Hanauer and Chalk 2012.

24. The Indian and Pakistani prime ministers met at the July 2015 Shanghai Cooperation Organization summit in Russia, their national security advisors held further talks, India's foreign minister visited Pakistan in early December 2015, and Prime Minister Modi visited Pakistan in late December 2015. In January 2016, while Pakistan-based militants attacked an Indian air force base, this did not disrupt the India-Pakistan dialogue because Pakistan declared that it would act against the group that was reportedly behind the attack, the Jaish-e-Mohammad.

25. In practice, militant attacks in Kashmir reduced considerably by the end of the first decade of the 2000s, partly due to Islamabad's reduced support for militants and partly because of India's improved counterterrorism and security measures. The number of Indian security personnel killed in these attacks was 800–1,000 each year in 1999–2002, and then 650 (2003), 530 (2004), 520 (2005), 350 (2006), 160 (2007), 70 (2008), 55 (2009), 36 (2010), 34 (2011), 16 (2012), 20 (2013), and 32 (2014). At the same time, attacks elsewhere in India by Islamist

extremists, some of whom had links with Pakistan, continued: fatalities (largely civilian) in such attacks were 73 (2005), 230 (2006, including 180 in train blasts in Mumbai on July 11), 60 (2007), 370 (2008, which included 160 fatalities in the November 26 Mumbai attacks), 5 (2009), 20 (2010), 42 (2011), 1 (2012), and 25 (2013). Source: South Asia Terrorism Portal.

Overall, analysts note that while Pakistani authorities cracked down on anti-Pakistan terror groups, Pakistani "schools, clerics, and some media outlets continue to churn out hardline narratives" about threats from India; that "the Pakistani state—and particularly the security establishment—often parrots" these narratives; and that "the [Pakistani] state has not severed its ties with terror groups such as the Haqqani network, Jaish-e-Mohammad, and Lashkar-e-Taiba that target Afghanistan and India" (Kugelman 2015). And the US State Department country reports on terrorism noted, in its 2014 report, that "LeT [Lashkar-e-Taiba] and its alias organizations continued to operate freely in Pakistan, and there were no indications that Pakistan took significant enforcement actions against the group."

26. The Bush administration had offered to finance the Indian troop deployments that were expected to cost US$300 million, to help India recover its investments in Iraq made under Saddam Hussein's regime, and to offer Indian firms a share of Iraqi economic reconstruction.

27. If New Delhi and Washington were the closest partners, as the optimists desired, then India's policies should have aligned to a high level with US preferences in a majority of cases—at least six of the twelve cases in this study. Conversely, if the US-India relationship was flagging, as skeptics suggested, then India's policies should have converged to a low or negligible extent with US preferences in a majority of the cases.

28. Thus, Indian officials noted that in the early 2010s, their government was faltering "both in terms of political administration and in terms of policy" and that governmental "decision-making came to a standstill." See Council on Foreign Relations 2015a.

29. Further, on about twelve select issues—related to human rights, nuclear arms control, Israeli-Palestine issues, and development—New Delhi regularly voted on the same side as the United States on just two of these issues, those related to development and to the right to life. See US Department of State 2014.

Bibliography

Albright Stonebridge Group. 2014. "Running on Empty: India's Defence Sector Procurements," newsletter, March 6.

Aspen Institute India. 2012. *India's Iran Conundrum: A Litmus Test for India's Foreign Policy.* Haryana, India: Aspen Institute.

Bagchi, Indrani. 2015. "To Get Around Nuclear Liability, Government Mulls an Insurance Fund," *Times of India,* January 7.

Bannerjee, Dipankar. 2013. "India." In *Providing Peacekeepers: The Politics, Challenges, and Future of United Nations Peacekeeping Contributions,* edited by Alex Bellamy and Paul Williams. New York: Oxford University Press.

Blackwill, Robert. 2005. "The India Imperative," *The National Interest,* 80.

Boggs, Robert, and Nicholas Burns. 2015. "Friends Without Benefits," *Foreign Affairs* 94 (1).

Brewster, David. 2012. *India as an Asia Pacific Power.* New York: Routledge.

Brewster, David. 2014. *India's Ocean: The Story of India's Bid for Regional Leadership.* Abingdon, Oxon: Routledge.

Brewster, David. 2015. "Indian Strategic Thinking about the Indian Ocean: Striving Toward Strategic Leadership," *India Review* 14 (2): 221–37.

The Brookings Institution. 2015. *The Second Modi-Obama Summit: Building the India-US Partnership.* Washington, DC: The Brookings Institution.

Burns, Nicholas. 2007. "America's Strategic Opportunity With India," *Foreign Affairs* 86 (6).

Business Standard. 2013. "Biden Visit Reveals Potential and Pitfalls of US-India Ties," July 24.

Center for Policy Research. 2012. *Nonalignment 2.0: A Foreign and Strategic Policy for India in the Twenty-First Century.* New Delhi: Center for Policy Research.

Chaudhuri, Pramit. 2014. "The US-India Defense Relationship: Strengthening Ties and Overcoming Challenges," National Bureau of Asian Research, July 1.

Chaudhuri, Rudra. 2014. *Forged in Crisis: India and the United States Since 1947.* New York: Oxford University Press.

Cohen, Stephen, P. R. Chari, and Pervaiz Iqbal Cheema. 2007. *Four Crises and a Peace Process.* Washington, DC: The Brookings Institution.

Coll, Steve. 2009. "The Back Channel: India and Pakistan's Secret Kashmir Talks," *The New Yorker*, March 2.

Collin, Koh Swee Lean. 2013. "ASEAN Perspectives on Naval Cooperation With India: Singapore and Vietnam," *India Review* 12 (3) (2013): 186–206.

Council on Foreign Relations. 2015a. "Transcript: C. Peter McColough Series on International Economics: A Conversation with Arun Jaitley," New York, June 18.

Council on Foreign Relations. 2015b. *Working with a Rising India: A Joint Venture for the New Century*, Independent Task Force Report No. 73.

Curtis, Lisa. 2011. "U.S.-India Counterterrorism Cooperation: Deepening the Partnership," testimony before the United States House of Representatives, Committee on Foreign Affairs, Subcommittee on Terrorism, Nonproliferation, and Trade, September 14.

Daniel, Donald, Patricia Taft, and Sharon Wiharta, eds. 2008. *Peace Operations: Trends, Progress, and Prospects.* Washington, DC: Georgetown University Press.

Darymple, William. 2013. *A Deadly Triangle: Afghanistan, Pakistan, and India.* Washington, DC: The Brookings Institution.

Economic Times. 2003. "India Not to Send Troops to Iraq," July 15.

Embassy of India. 2000. "Joint Statement of the US-India Peacekeeping Group." Washington, DC: Embassy of India, September.

Fair, C. Christine. 2007. "India and Iran: New Delhi's Balancing Act," *The Washington Quarterly* 30 (3): 145–59.

Fitch, Brianna, Melissa Hersh, Rick Nelson, Ally Pregulman, and Rob Wise. 2013. *U.S.-India Homeland Security Cooperation: Building a Lasting Partnership via Transportation Sector Security*. Washington, DC: Center for Strategic and International Studies.

Gates, Robert. 2009. "America's Security Role in the Asia-Pacific," speech at the 8th IISS Asia Security Summit, Shangri-La Dialogue, Singapore, May 30.

Goel, Anish. 2014. "Why the US and India Are Trading Fewer Goods and More Insults," *Foreign Policy*, April 3.

Gould, Harold, and Sumit Ganguly, eds. 1992. *The Hope and the Reality: US-India Relations from Roosevelt to Reagan*. Boulder, CO: Westview Press.

Gupta, Saurabh. 2014. "A US-India Strategic Reset: Getting Back to Basics," PacNet #67, August 14.

Hagerty, Devin. 2006. "Are We Present at the Creation: Alliance Theory and the Indo-US Strategic Convergence." In *US-Indian Strategic Cooperation into the 21st Century: More Than Words,* edited by Sumit Ganguly, Brian Shoup, and Andrew Scobell. New York: Routledge, 11–30.

Hanauer, Larry, and Peter Chalk. 2012. *India's and Pakistan's Strategies in Afghanistan*. Washington, DC: RAND.

Heginbotham, Eric, and George Gilroy. 2012. *Chinese and Indian Strategic Behavior: Growing Power and Alarm*. Cambridge, UK: Cambridge University Press.

The Hindu. 2014. "Centre Concedes Giving Training to Lankan Navy," March 26.

The Hindu. 2015. "N-deal Logjam Cleared: Modi, Obama Agree Not to Dilute Liability Law," January 26.

The Indian Express. 2013. "BJP Slams Pakistan Parliament Resolution Against Afzal Guru's Hanging," March 15.

International Crisis Group. 2012. "Pakistan's Relations with India: Beyond Kashmir?" *Asia Report* no. 224, May 3.

IISS (International Institute of Strategic Studies). 2014. *The Military Balance 2014*. London: International Institute for Strategic Studies.

Jaishankar, Dhruva. 2014. "From Bombay to Jerusalem: With the Crisis in Iraq Worsening, How Involved Should India Get in the Middle East?" *Foreign Policy*, July 2.

Kifner, John. 2003. "In Rebuff to US, India Says It Won't Send Troops to Iraq," *New York Times*, July 14.

Kronstadt, Alan, and Sonia Pinto. 2013. *U.S.-India Security Relations: Strategic Issues*. Washington, DC: Congressional Research Service, January 24.

Kugelman, Michael. 2015. "Pakistan's Failed War on Ideology." The South Asia Channel, *Foreign Policy*, December 8.

Kugelman, Michael, and Robert Hathaway. 2013. *Pakistan-India Trade: What Needs to Be Done? What Does It Matter?* Washington, DC: Woodrow Wilson Center.

Kumaraswamy, P. R. 2008. "Delhi: Between Tehran and Washington," *Middle East Quarterly* 15 (1): 41–47.

Kundnani, Hans. 2015. "Leaving the West Behind: Germany Looks East," *Foreign Affairs* 94: 1.

Kux, Dennis. 1993. *Estranged Democracies: India and the United States, 1941–1991*. Washington, DC: National Defense University Press.

Lancaster, John. 2005. "India Takes a Major Role in Sri Lanka Relief Effort," *Washington Post*, January 20.

Latif, S. Amer. 2012. *US-India Defense Trade: Opportunities for Deepening the Partnership*. Washington, DC: Center for Strategic and International Studies.

Lavoy, Peter, and Joshua White. 2015. "Sustaining Ambition in the U.S.-India Relationship," *Foreign Policy*, February 4.

Limaye, Satu. 1993. *U.S.-Indian Relations: The Pursuit of Accommodation*. Boulder, CO: Westview Press.

Markey, Daniel. 2013. *No Exit from Pakistan*. New York: Cambridge University Press.

McMahon, Robert. 1994. *The Cold War on the Periphery: The United States, India, and Pakistan*. New York: Columbia University Press.

Ministry of External Affairs (India). 2014. "Tokyo Declaration for India-Japan Special Strategic and Global Partnership," Ministry of External Affairs, Government of India, press release, September 1, 2014.

Ministry of External Affairs (India). 2015. "Frequently Asked Questions and Answers on Civil Liability for Nuclear Damage Act 2010 and Related Issues," Ministry of External Affairs, Government of India, press release, February 8.

Mohan, C. Raja. 2012. *Samundra Mathan: Sino-Indian Rivalry in the Indo-Pacific*. Washington, DC: Carnegie Endowment for International Peace.

Montgomery, Evan. 2013. "Competitive Strategies Against Continental Powers: The Geopolitics of Sino-Indian-American Relations," *Journal of Strategic Studies* 36 (1): 76–100.

Mukherjee, Anit, and Manohar Thyagraj. 2012. "Competing Exceptionalisms: US-India Defence Relationship," *Journal of Defence Studies* 6 (2): 12–28.

Mullen, Rani. 2016. "India-Afghanistan Relations." In *Engaging the World: Indian Foreign Policy Since 1947,* edited by Sumit Ganguly. New Delhi: Oxford University Press.

Nadir, Khalid. 2014. "Old Habits, New Consequences: Pakistan's Posture Toward Afghanistan Since 2001," *International Security* 39 (2): 132–68.

Nayan, Rajiv. 2011. "Indian Chemical Export Controls System and the Australia Group," *CBW Magazine*, June.

Observer Research Foundation. 2014a. *The Importance of Indo-Omani Relations,* June 21.

Observer Research Foundation. 2014b. *Indo-US Cooperation on Internet Governance & Cybersecurity*, October 2014.

O'Hanlon, Michael. 2013. "Hope in 'A Deadly Triangle' of Afghanistan, Pakistan and India," The Brookings Institution, July 3.

Olapally, Deepa. 2005. *US-India Relations: The Ties That Bind.* Washington, DC: George Washington University, The Sigur Center Asia Papers series.

Panagariya, Arvind. 2012. "A Leader of Substance: Along with Narasimha Rao, Atal Bihari Vajpayee Laid the Foundation of New India," *Times of India*, December 25.

Pant, Harsh. 2007. "India's Relations with Iran: Much Ado about Nothing," *The Washington Quarterly* 34 (1): 61–74.

Pant, Harsh, and Julie Super. 2015. "India's 'Non-Alignment' Conundrum: A Twentieth-Century Policy in a Changing World," *International Affairs* 91 (4): 747–64.

Paul, T. V., James Wirtz, and Michel Fortmann. 2014. *Balance of Power: Theory and Practice in the 21st Century.* Stanford, CA: Stanford University Press.

Perkovich, George. 2010. "Toward Realistic US-India Relations," Washington, DC: Carnegie Endowment for International Peace.

Price, Gareth. 2013. *India's Policy Toward Afghanistan.* London: Chatham House.

Ranasinghe, Sergei DeSilva. 2014. "Potent and Capable: India's Transformational 21st Century Navy," *Future Directions* (Australia), May 3.

Reidel, Bruce. 2013. "Pakistan, Taliban, and the Afghan Quagmire," *The Diplomatist*, August 24.

Rice, Condoleezza. 2000. "Promoting the National Interest," *Foreign Affairs* 79 (1): 45–62.

Rice, Condoleezza. 2006. "Our Opportunity with India," *The Washington Post*, March 13.

Rice, Condoleezza. 2011. *No Higher Honor: A Memoir of My Years in Washington*. New York: Crown.

Samaranayake, Nilanthi, Satu Limaye, Dmitry Gorenburg, Catherine Lea, and Thomas Bowditch. 2013. *U.S.-India Security Burden-Sharing? The Potential for Coordinated Capacity-Building in the Indian Ocean*. Washington, DC: Center for Naval Analysis.

Schaffer, Teresita. 2009. *India and the United States in the 21st Century: Reinventing Partnership*. Washington, DC: Center for Strategic and International Studies.

Schaffer, Teresita, and Joan Rohlfing. 2011. *India and the Nonproliferation System*. Washington, DC: Nuclear Threat Initiative.

Schweller, Randall. 2004. "Unanswered Threats: A Neoclassical Realist Theory of Underbalancing," *International Security* 29 (2): 159–201.

Scott, David. 2013. "India's Aspirations and Strategy for the Indian Ocean—Securing the Waves?" *Journal of Strategic Studies* 36 (4): 484–511.

Sethi, Abheet Singh. 2015. "82% Roads Along China Border Unfinished," *Gateway House*, Mumbai, June 29.

Shukla, P. P., ed. 2014. *India-US Partnership: Asian Challenges and Beyond*. New Delhi, Wisdom Tree.

Shukla, Vijay. 2005. "Indian Naval Diplomacy: Post Tsunami," Institute of Peace and Conflict Studies, New Delhi: IPCS Article 1640, February 8.

Sibal, Kanwal. 2012. "Strategic Relations Suit India," *India Today*, December 26.

Sidhu, Waheguru Pal Singh, Pratap Bhanu Mehta, and Bruce Jones, eds. 2013. *Shaping the Emerging World: India and the Multilateral Order*. Washington, DC: The Brookings Institution.

Smith, Jeff. 2014. *Cold Peace: China-India Rivalry in the Twenty-First Century*. Lanham, MD: Lexington Books.

Sorenson, David, and Pia Christina Wood, eds. 2005. *The Politics of Peacekeeping in the Post–Cold War Era*. New York: Psychology Press.

South Asia Terrorism Portal, New Delhi. www.satp.org

Suryanarayan, V. 2013. "India and Singapore: Defence Cooperation on the Upswing," Institute of Peace and Conflict Studies, New Delhi: IPCS Article 3987, June 10.

Talbott, Strobe. 2004. *Engaging India.* Washington, DC: Brookings Institution Press.

Tellis, Ashley. 2011. *Dogfight: India's Medium Multi-Role Combat Aircraft Decision.* Washington, DC: Carnegie Endowment for International Peace.

Times of India. 2013a. "Pak Troops Kill Two Jawans, Behead, Mutilate, One of Them," January 9.

Times of India. 2013b. "Sarabjit Singh Butchered By Our Enemies," May 4.

Thompson, Julia. 2015. "Growing Violence Along the Kashmir Divide," Stimson Center, August 6.

Twinning, Daniel. 2014. "Building U.S. Partnerships for the 21st Century: The Case of (and for) India." In *Strategic Asia 2014–15: US Alliances and Partnerships at the Center of Global Power,* edited by Ashley Tellis. Seattle, WA: National Bureau of Asian Research.

US Department of State. 2013. "Secretary Kerry's Meeting with Pakistani Prime Minister Nawaz Sharif," October 20.

US Department of State. 2014. *Voting Practices in the United Nations.*

US Embassy. 2005. "GOI Updates on Export Controls during HTCG," US Embassy, New Delhi, December 8.

US Embassy. 2007. "Assistant Secretary Boucher and Gaitri Kumar Review Bilateral State-of-Play," US Embassy, New Delhi, April 11.

Vickery, Raymond. 2011. *The Eagle and the Elephant: Strategic Aspects of US-India Economic Engagement.* Washington, DC: Johns Hopkins.

von Hlatsky, Stefanie. 2013. *American Allies in Times of War: The Great Asymmetry.* New York: Oxford University Press.

The White House. 2015a. "US-India Joint Statement: Shared Effort, Progress for All," January 25.

The White House. 2015b. "Joint Statement on the First U.S.-India Strategic and Commercial Dialogue," September 22.

Wilkins, Thomas. 2012. "'Alignment', Not 'Alliance'—The Shifting Paradigm of International Security Cooperation: Toward a Conceptual Taxonomy of Alignment," *Review of International Studies* 38 (1): 53–76.

Acknowledgments

Research for this study was supported by an East-West Center Asia Studies fellowship. The author would like to thank all at the East-West Center office in Washington, DC for their assistance while the first draft of this study was written; Satu Limaye and Stephen Cohen, who offered helpful comments during a presentation of this study in the summer, 2014; and Marcus Mietzner and the reviewers of this manuscript, who offered additional useful insights. The author also acknowledges inputs from participants in workshops where sections of this paper were discussed.

www.ingramcontent.com/pod-product-compliance
Lightning Source LLC
Chambersburg PA
CBHW050602280326
41933CB00011B/1953